Ben Stacy Jerrik (Ed.)

Act Of Uniformity Amendment Act 1872

Ben Stacy Jerrik (Ed.)

Act Of Uniformity Amendment Act 1872

Parliament of the United Kingdom, Legislature, Parliament

Part Press

Imprint

Publisher:
Part Press is a trademark of
International Book Market Service Ltd., 17 Rue Meldrum, Beau Bassin, 1713-01 Mauritius
Email: info@bookmarketservice.com
Website: www.bookmarketservice.com

Published in 2013

Printed in: U.S.A., U.K., Germany. This book was not produced in Mauritius.

ISBN: 978-620-1-67192-8

Contents

Articles

Act_of_Uniformity_Amendment_Act_1872 1

Parliament_of_the_United_Kingdom 1

Legislature 14

Parliament 15

Book_of_Common_Prayer 29

Act_of_Parliament 47

Burial_Laws_Amendment_Act_1880 53

References

Article Sources and Contributors 55

Image Sources, Licenses and Contributors 57

Act_of_Uniformity_Amendment_Act_1872

The **Act of Uniformity Amendment Act 1872** (35 & 36 Vict. c. 35), sometimes called the *Shortened Services Act*, was an Act of the Parliament of the United Kingdom that amended some of the provisions of the English Act of Uniformity 1662.

It allowed certain modifications[1]

- a shortened form of Morning and Evening Prayer on week days
- on special occasions approved by the Ordinary special forms of service, provided that they contain nothing, except anthems or hymns, which did form part of the Holy Scriptures or the Book of Common Prayer
- additional forms of service on Sundays and Holy-days in addition to the regular services, approved by the Ordinary.
- the use of Morning Prayer, the Litany, and the Communion Service as separate services and in varying order
- sermons or lectures without the common prayers or services appointed by the Prayer Book

See also

- Prayer Book (Tables of Lessons) Act 1871
- Burial Laws Amendment Act 1880

References

[1] REPORT OF THE ROYAL COMMISSION ON ECCLESIASTICAL DISCIPLINE (http://anglicanhistory.org/pwra/rced2.html) 1906

Parliament_of_the_United_Kingdom

The **Parliament of the United Kingdom of Great Britain and Northern Ireland**,[1] commonly known as the **British Parliament**, **Westminster Parliament** or simply "Westminster", is the supreme legislative body in the United Kingdom, British Crown dependencies and British overseas territories. It is located in the Palace of Westminster, Westminster, London. Parliament alone possesses legislative supremacy and thereby ultimate power over all other political bodies in the UK and its territories. At its head is the Sovereign, Queen Elizabeth II.

The parliament is bicameral, with an upper house, the House of Lords, and a lower house, the House of Commons.[2] The Queen is the third component of the legislature.[3] [4] The House of Lords includes two different types of members: the Lords Spiritual (the senior bishops of the Church of England) and the Lords Temporal (members of the Peerage) whose members are not elected by the population at large, but are appointed by the Sovereign on the advice of the Prime Minister.[5] Prior to the opening of the Supreme Court in October 2009 the House of Lords also performed a judicial role through the Law Lords.

The House of Commons is a democratically elected chamber with elections held at least every five years.[6] The two Houses meet in separate chambers in the Palace of Westminster (commonly known as the Houses of Parliament), in London. By constitutional convention, all government ministers, including the Prime Minister, are members of the House of Commons or, less often, the House of Lords, and are thereby accountable to the respective branches of the legislature.

The Parliament of Great Britain was formed in 1707 following the ratification of the Treaty of Union both by the Parliament of England and by the Parliament of Scotland passing Acts of Union. However, in practice the parliament was a continuation of the English parliament with the addition of Scottish MPs and peers. Parliament was further enlarged by the ratification by the Parliament of Great Britain and the Parliament of Ireland of the Act of Union (1800), which abolished the Irish Parliament; this added 100 Irish members to the Commons and 32 to the Lords to create the Parliament of the United Kingdom of Great Britain and Ireland.

It has been called "the mother of parliaments", its democratic institutions having set the standards for many democracies throughout the world,[7] and the United Kingdom parliament is the largest Anglophone legislative body in the world.[8] However, the originator of the expression "mother of parliaments", John Bright, used it in reference to England, and not to her parliament.[9]

In theory, supreme legislative power is vested in the Queen-in-Parliament; in practice in modern times, real power is vested in the House of Commons, as the Sovereign generally acts on the advice of the Prime Minister, and the powers of the House of Lords have been limited.[10]

History

For earlier background see Parliament of England, Parliament of Scotland, Parliament of Great Britain, and Parliament of Ireland.

Parliament of the United Kingdom of Great Britain and Ireland

The United Kingdom of Great Britain and Ireland was created in 1801 by the merger of the Kingdoms of Great Britain and Ireland under the Act of Union.

The principle of ministerial responsibility to the lower House did not develop until the 19th century—the House of Lords was superior to the House of Commons both in theory and in practice. Members of the House of Commons were elected in an antiquated electoral system, under which constituencies of vastly different sizes existed. Thus, the borough of Old Sarum, with seven voters, could elect two members, as could the borough of Dunwich, which had completely disappeared into the sea due to land erosion.

In many cases, members of the Upper House also controlled tiny constituencies, known as pocket or rotten boroughs, and could ensure the election of their relatives or supporters. Many seats in the House of Commons were "owned" by the Lords. After the reforms of the 19th century, beginning with the Reform Act 1832, the electoral system in the lower House was much more regularised. No longer dependent on the upper House for their seats, members of the House of Commons began to grow more assertive.

The supremacy of the British House of Commons was established in the early 20th century. In 1909, the Commons passed the so-called "People's Budget", which made numerous changes to the taxation system in a manner detrimental to wealthy landowners. The House of Lords, which consisted mostly of powerful landowners, rejected the Budget. On the basis of the Budget's popularity and the Lords' consequent unpopularity, the Liberal Party narrowly won two general elections in 1910.

Parliament at night, with the London Eye visible at right.

Using the result as a mandate, the Liberal Prime Minister, Herbert Henry Asquith, introduced the Parliament bill, which sought to restrict the powers of the House of Lords. (He did not reintroduce the land tax provision of the People's Budget). When the Lords refused to pass the bill, Asquith countered with a promise extracted from the King in secret before the second general election of 1910 and requested the creation of several hundred Liberal peers so as to erase the Conservative majority in the House of Lords. In the face of such a threat, the House of Lords narrowly passed the bill.

The Parliament Act 1911, as it became, prevented the Lords from blocking a money bill (a bill dealing with taxation), and allowed them to delay any other bill for a maximum of three sessions (reduced to two sessions in

1949), after which it could become law over their objections. However, regardless of the Parliament Acts of 1911 and 1949, the House of Lords has always retained the unrestricted power to be able to block and veto any bill outright which attempts to extend the life of a parliament.[11]

Parliament of the United Kingdom of Great Britain and Northern Ireland

The Government of Ireland Act 1920 created the parliaments of Northern Ireland and Southern Ireland and reduced the representation of both parts at Westminster. (The number of Northern Ireland seats was increased again after the introduction of direct rule in 1973.) The Irish Free State became independent in 1922, and in 1927 parliament was renamed the *Parliament of the United Kingdom of Great Britain and Northern Ireland.*

Further reforms to the House of Lords have been made during the 20th century. The Life Peerages Act 1958 authorised the regular creation of life peerage dignities. By the 1960s, the regular creation of hereditary peerage dignities had ceased; thereafter, almost all new peers were life peers only.

More recently, the House of Lords Act 1999 removed the automatic right of hereditary peers to sit in the Upper House (although it made an exception for 92 of them on a temporary basis, to be elected to life-terms by the other hereditary peers with by-elections upon their death). The House of Lords is now a chamber that is subordinate to the House of Commons. Additionally, the Constitutional Reform Act 2005 led to abolition of the judicial functions of the House of Lords with the creation of the new Supreme Court of the United Kingdom in October 2009.

Composition and powers

The legislative authority, the Crown-in-Parliament, has three separate elements: the Monarch, the House of Lords, and the House of Commons. No individual may be a member of both Houses, and members of the House of Lords are legally barred from voting in elections for members of the House of Commons.

Royal Assent of the Monarch is required for all Bills to become law, and certain Delegated Legislation must be made by the Monarch by Order in Council. The Crown also has executive powers which do not depend on Parliament, through prerogative powers, which include among others the ability to make treaties, declare war, award honours, and appoint officers and civil servants. In practice these are always exercised by the monarch on the advice of the Prime Minister and the other ministers of HM Government. The Prime Minister and government are directly accountable to Parliament, through its control of public finances, and to the public, through election of Members of Parliament.

The Monarch also chooses the Prime Minister, who then forms a government from members of the houses of parliament. This must be someone who could command a majority in a confidence vote in the House of Commons. In the recent past the monarch has had to make a judgment, as in the appointment of Alec Douglas-Home in 1963 when it was thought that the incumbent Prime Minister, Harold Macmillan, had become ill with terminal cancer. However, today the monarch is advised by the outgoing Prime Minister as to whom she should offer the position next.

The Upper House is formally styled *The Right Honourable The Lords Spiritual and Temporal in Parliament Assembled*, the Lords Spiritual being bishops of the Church of England and the Lords Temporal being Peers of the Realm. The Lords Spiritual and Lords Temporal are considered separate "estates", but they sit, debate and vote together.

Since the Parliament Acts 1911 and 1949, the powers of the House of Lords have been very much less than those of the House of Commons. All bills except money bills are debated and voted upon in House of Lords; however by voting against a bill, the House of Lords can only delay it for a maximum of two parliamentary sessions over a year. After this time, the House of Commons can force the Bill through without the Lords' consent under the Parliament Acts. The House of Lords can also hold the government to account through questions to government ministers and the operation of a small number of select committees. The highest court in England & Wales and Northern Ireland used to be a committee of the House of Lords, but it became an independent supreme court in 2009.

The Lords Spiritual formerly included all of the senior clergymen of the Church of England—archbishops, bishops, abbots and mitred priors. Upon the Dissolution of the Monasteries under Henry VIII the abbots and mitred priors lost their positions in Parliament. All diocesan bishops continued to sit in Parliament, but the Bishopric of Manchester Act 1847, and later acts, provide that only the 26 most senior are Lords Spiritual. These always include the incumbents of the "five great sees", namely the Archbishop of Canterbury, the Archbishop of York, the Bishop of London, the Bishop of Durham and the Bishop of Winchester. The remaining 21 Lords Spiritual are the most senior diocesan bishops, ranked in order of consecration.

The Lords Temporal are all members of the Peerage. Formerly, they were hereditary peers. The right of some hereditary peers to sit in Parliament was not automatic: after Scotland and England united into Great Britain in 1707, it was provided that all peers whose dignities had been created by English Kings could sit in Parliament, but those whose dignities had been created by Scottish Kings were to elect a limited number of "representative peers". A similar arrangement was made in respect of Ireland when it was united with Great Britain in 1801, but when southern Ireland left the United Kingdom in 1922 the election of Irish representative peers ceased. By the Peerage Act 1963, the election of Scottish representative peers also ended, and all Scottish peers were granted the right to sit in Parliament. Under the House of Lords Act 1999, only life peerages (that is to say, peerage dignities which cannot be inherited) automatically entitle their holders to seats in the House of Lords. Of the hereditary peers, only 92—the Earl Marshal, the Lord Great Chamberlain and the 90 elected by other peers—retain their seats in the House.

The Commons, the last of the "estates" of the Kingdom, are represented in the House of Commons, which is formally styled *The Honourable The Commons in Parliament Assembled* (*commons* coming not from the term *commoner*, but from *commune*, the old French term for a district). The House currently consists of 650 members. Each "Member of Parliament" or "MP" is chosen by a single constituency according to the First-Past-the-Post electoral system. Universal adult suffrage exists for those 18 and over; citizens of the United Kingdom, and those of the Republic of Ireland and Commonwealth nations resident in the United Kingdom are qualified to vote, unless they are in prison at the time of the elections. The term of members of the House of Commons depends on the term of Parliament, a maximum of five years; a general election, during which all the seats are contested, occurs after each dissolution (see below).

All legislation must be passed by the House of Commons to become law and it controls taxation and the supply of money to the government. Government ministers (including the Prime Minister) must regularly answer questions in the House of Commons and there are a number of select committees that scrutinise particular issues and the workings of the government. There are also mechanisms that allow members of the House of Commons to bring to the attention of the government particular issues affecting their constituents.

State Opening

The State Opening of Parliament is an annual event that marks the commencement of a session of the Parliament of the United Kingdom. It is held in the House of Lords Chamber, usually in November or December,[12] or in a general election year, when the new Parliament first assembles.

The monarch reads a prepared speech, known as the Speech from the Throne, outlining the Government's agenda for the coming year. The speech is not written by the monarch, but rather by the Cabinet, and reflects the legislative agenda for which they seek the agreement of both Houses of Parliament.

After the monarch leaves, each Chamber proceeds to the consideration of an "Address in Reply to Her Majesty's Gracious Speech." But first, each House considers a bill *pro forma* to symbolise their right to deliberate independently of the monarch. In the House of Lords, the bill is called the *Select Vestries Bill*, while the Commons equivalent is the *Outlawries Bill*. The Bills are considered for the sake of form only, and do not make any actual progress.

Procedure

See also the stages of a bill section in Acts of Parliament in the United Kingdom

Both houses of the British Parliament are presided over by a speaker, the Speaker of the House for the Commons and the Lord Speaker in the House of Lords.

For the Commons, the approval of the Sovereign is theoretically required before the election of the Speaker becomes valid, but it is, by modern convention, always granted. The Speaker's place may be taken by three deputies, known as the Chairman, First Deputy Chairman and Second Deputy Chairman of Ways and Means. (They take their name from the Committee of Ways and Means, of which they were once presiding officers, but which no longer exists.)

Prior to July 2006, the House of Lords was presided over by a Lord Chancellor (a Cabinet member), whose influence as Speaker was very limited (whilst the powers belonging to the Speaker of the House of Commons are vast). However, as part of the Constitutional Reform Act 2005, the position of Speaker of the House of Lords (as it is termed in the Act) was separated from the office of Lord Chancellor (the office which has control over the judiciary as a whole), though the Lords remain largely self-governing. Decisions on points of order and on the disciplining of unruly members are made by the whole body in the Upper House, but by the Speaker alone in the Lower House. Speeches in the House of Lords are addressed to the House as a whole (using the words "My Lords"), but those in the House of Commons are addressed to the Speaker alone (using "Mr Speaker" or "Madam Speaker"). Speeches may be made to both Houses simultaneously. As of June 2011, Barack Obama was the most recent person to address both Houses.[13]

Both Houses may decide questions by voice vote; members shout out "Aye" and "No" in the Commons—or "Content" and "Not-Content" in the Lords—and the presiding officer declares the result. The pronouncement of either Speaker may be challenged, and a recorded vote (known as a division) demanded. (The Speaker of the House of Commons may choose to overrule a frivolous request for a division, but the Lord Speaker does not have that power). In each House, a division requires members to file into one of the two lobbies alongside the Chamber; their names are recorded by clerks, and their votes are counted as they exit the lobbies to re-enter the Chamber. The Speaker of the House of Commons is expected to be non-partisan, and does not cast a vote except in the case of a tie; the Lord Speaker, however, votes along with the other Lords.

Both Houses normally conduct their business in public, and there are galleries where visitors may sit.

Term

Following a general election, a new Parliamentary session begins. Parliament is formally summoned 40 days in advance by the Sovereign, who is the source of parliamentary authority. On the day indicated by the Sovereign's proclamation, the two Houses assemble in their respective chambers. The Commons are then summoned to the House of Lords, where Lords Commissioners (representatives of the Sovereign) instruct them to elect a Speaker. The Commons perform the election; on the next day, they return to the House of Lords, where the Lords Commissioners confirm the election and grant the new Speaker the royal approval in the Sovereign's name.

The business of Parliament for the next few days of its session involves the taking of the oaths of allegiance. Once a majority of the members have taken the oath in each House, the State Opening of Parliament may occur. The Lords take their seats in the House of Lords Chamber, the Commons appear at the Bar (immediately outside the Chamber), and the Sovereign takes his or her seat on the throne. The Sovereign then reads the Speech from the Throne—the content of which is determined by the Ministers of the Crown—outlining the Government's legislative agenda for the upcoming year. Thereafter, each House proceeds to the transaction of legislative business.

By custom, before considering the Government's legislative agenda, a bill is introduced *pro forma* in each House—the Select Vestries Bill in the House of Lords and the Outlawries Bill in the House of Commons. These bills do not become laws; they are ceremonial indications of the power of each House to debate independently of the Crown. After the *pro forma* bill is introduced, each House debates the content of the Speech from the Throne for several days. Once each House formally sends its reply to the Speech, legislative business may commence, appointing committees, electing officers, passing resolutions and considering legislation.

A session of Parliament is brought to an end by a prorogation. There is a ceremony similar to the State Opening, but much less well-known. Normally, the Sovereign does not personally attend the prorogation ceremony in the House of Lords; he or she is represented by Lords Commissioners. The next session of Parliament begins under the procedures described above, but it is not necessary to conduct another election of a Speaker or take the oaths of allegiance afresh at the beginning of such subsequent sessions. Instead, the State Opening of Parliament proceeds directly. To avoid the delay of opening a new session in the event of an emergency during the long summer recess, Parliament is no longer prorogued beforehand, but only after the Houses have reconvened in the autumn; the State Opening follows a few days later.

Each Parliament comes to an end, after a number of sessions, in anticipation of a general election. Parliament is dissolved by virtue of the Fixed-term Parliaments Act 2011. Prior to it, dissolution was effected by the Sovereign, always on the advice of the Prime Minister. The Prime Minister could seek dissolution because the time was politically advantageous to his or her party. If the Prime Minister loses the support of the House of Commons, Parliament will dissolve and a new election will be held. Parliaments can also be dissolved if two thirds of the House of Commons votes for an early election.

Originally there was no fixed limit on the length of a Parliament, but the Triennial Act 1694 set the maximum duration at three years. As the frequent elections were deemed inconvenient, the Septennial Act 1715 extended the maximum to seven years, but the Parliament Act 1911 reduced it to five. During the Second World War, the term was temporarily extended to ten years by Acts of Parliament. Since the end of the war the maximum has remained five years. Modern Parliaments, however, rarely continued for the maximum duration; normally, they were dissolved earlier. For instance, the 52nd, which assembled in 1997, was dissolved after four years. The Septennial Act was repealed by the Fixed-term Parliaments Act.

Formerly, the demise of the Sovereign automatically brought a Parliament to an end, the Crown being seen as the *caput, principium, et finis* (beginning, basis and end) of the body, but this is no longer the case. The first change was during the reign of William and Mary, when it was seen to be inconvenient to have no Parliament at a time when succession to the Crown could be disputed, and an act was passed that provided that a Parliament was to continue for six months after the death of a Sovereign, unless dissolved earlier. (This provision is today contained in the Representation of the People Act 1867.)

After each Parliament concludes, the Crown issues writs to hold a general election and elect new members of the House of Commons though membership of the House of Lords does not change due to dissolution.

Legislative functions

Laws can be made by Acts of the United Kingdom Parliament. While Acts can apply to the whole of the United Kingdom including Scotland, due to the continuing separation of Scots law many Acts do not apply to Scotland and are either matched by equivalent Acts that apply to Scotland alone or, since 1999, by legislation set by the Scottish Parliament relating to devolved matters.

Parliament meets in the Palace of Westminster.

This has led to a paradox known as the West Lothian question. The existence of a devolved Scottish Parliament means that while Westminster MPs from Scotland may vote directly on matters that affect English constituencies, they may not have much power over their laws affecting their own constituency. While any Act of the Scottish Parliament may be overturned, amended or ignored by Westminster, in practice this has yet to happen. Furthermore, the existence of the Legislative Consent Motion enables English MPs to vote on issues nominally devolved to Scotland, as part of United Kingdom legislation. Since there is no devolved "English Parliament", the converse is not true.

Laws, in draft form known as bills, may be introduced by any member of either House, but usually a bill is introduced by a Minister of the Crown. A bill introduced by a Minister is known as a "Government Bill"; one introduced by another member is called a "Private Member's Bill". A different way of categorising bills involves the subject. Most bills, involving the general public, are called "Public Bills". A bill that seeks to grant special rights to an individual or small group of individuals, or a body such as a local authority, is called a "Private Bill". A Public Bill which affects private rights (in the way a Private Bill would) is called a "Hybrid Bill".

Private Members' Bills make up the majority of bills, but are far less likely to be passed than government bills. There are three methods for an MP to introduce a Private Member's Bill. The Private Members' Ballot (once per Session) put names into a ballot, and those who win are given time to propose a bill. The Ten Minute Rule is another method, where MPs are granted ten minutes to outline the case for a new piece of legislation. Standing Order 57 is the third method, which allows a bill to be introduced without debate if a day's notice is given to the Table Office. Filibustering is a danger, as an opponent to a bill can waste much of the limited time allotted to it. Private Members' Bills have no chance of success if the current government opposes them, but they are used in moral issues: the bills to decriminalise homosexuality and abortion were Private Members' Bills, for example. Governments can sometimes attempt to use Private Members' Bills to pass things it would rather not be associated with. "Handout bills" are bills which a government hands to MPs who win Private Members' Ballots.

Each Bill goes through several stages in each House. The first stage, called the first reading, is a formality. At the second reading, the general principles of the bill are debated, and the House may vote to reject the bill, by not passing the motion "That the Bill be now read a second time". Defeats of Government Bills are extremely rare, the last being in 2005.

Following the second reading, the bill is sent to a committee. In the House of Lords, the Committee of the Whole House or the Grand Committee are used. Each consists of all members of the House; the latter operates under special procedures, and is used only for uncontroversial bills. In the House of Commons, the bill is usually committed to a Public Bill Committee, consisting of between 16 and 50 members, but the Committee of the Whole House is used for important legislation. Several other types of committees, including Select Committees, may be used, but rarely. A committee considers the bill clause by clause, and reports the bill as amended to the House, where further detailed consideration ("consideration stage" or "report stage") occurs. However, a practice which used to be called the *kangaroo* (Standing Order 32) allows the Speaker to select which amendments are debated. This device is also used under Standing Order 89 by the committee chairman, to restrict debate in committee.

Once the House has considered the bill, the third reading follows. In the House of Commons, no further amendments may be made, and the passage of the motion "That the Bill be now read a third time" is passage of the whole bill. In the House of Lords further amendments to the bill may be moved. After the passage of the third reading motion, the House of Lords must vote on the motion "That the Bill do now pass." Following its passage in one House, the bill is sent to the other House. If passed in identical form by both Houses, it may be presented for the Sovereign's Assent. If one House passes amendments that the other will not agree to, and the two Houses cannot resolve their disagreements, the bill fails.

However, since the passage of the Parliament Act 1911 the power of the House of Lords to reject bills passed by the House of Commons has been restricted, and further restrictions were placed by the Parliament Act 1949. If the House of Commons passes a public bill in two successive sessions, and the House of Lords rejects it both times, the Commons may direct that the bill be presented to the Sovereign for his or her Assent, disregarding the rejection of the Bill in the House of Lords. In each case, the bill must be passed by the House of Commons at least one calendar month before the end of the session. The provision does not apply to bills originated in the House of Lords, to bills seeking to extend the duration of a Parliament beyond five years, or to Private Bills. A special procedure applies in relation to bills classified by the Speaker of the House of Commons as "Money Bills". A Money Bill concerns *solely* national taxation or public funds; the Speaker's certificate is deemed conclusive under all circumstances. If the House of Lords fails to pass a Money Bill within one month of its passage in the House of Commons, the Lower House may direct that the Bill be submitted for the Sovereign's Assent immediately.

Even before the passage of the Parliament Acts, the Commons possessed pre-eminence in cases of financial matters. By ancient custom, the House of Lords may not introduce a bill relating to taxation or Supply, nor amend a bill so as to insert a provision relating to taxation or Supply, nor amend a Supply Bill in any way. The House of Commons is free to waive this privilege, and sometimes does so to allow the House of Lords to pass amendments with financial implications. The House of Lords remains free to reject bills relating to Supply and taxation, but may be overruled easily if the bills are Money Bills. (A bill relating to revenue and Supply may not be a Money Bill if, for example, it includes subjects other than national taxation and public funds).

The last stage of a bill involves the granting of the Royal Assent. Theoretically, the Sovereign may either grant the Royal Assent (that is, make the bill a law) or withhold it (that is, veto the bill). Under modern conventions the Sovereign always grants the Royal Assent, in the Norman French words "La Reyne le veult" (the Queen wishes it; "Le roy" instead in the case of a king). The last refusal to grant the Assent was in 1708, when Queen Anne withheld her Assent from a bill "for the settling of Militia in Scotland", in the words "La reyne s'avisera" (the Queen will think it over).

Thus, every bill obtains the assent of all three components of Parliament before it becomes law (except where the House of Lords is over-ridden under the Parliament Acts 1911 and 1949). The words "BE IT ENACTED by the Queen's [King's] most Excellent Majesty, by and with the advice and consent of the Lords Spiritual and Temporal, and Commons, in this present Parliament assembled, and by the authority of the same, as follows:-", or, where the House of Lords' authority has been overridden by use of the Parliament Acts, the words "BE IT ENACTED by The Queen's [King's] most Excellent Majesty, by and with the advice and consent of the Commons in this present Parliament assembled, in accordance with the provisions of the Parliament Acts 1911 and 1949, and by the authority of the same, as follows:-" appear near the beginning of each Act of Parliament. These words are known as the enacting formula.

Judicial functions

Prior to the creation of the Supreme Court of the United Kingdom in October 2009, Parliament also used to perform several judicial functions. The Queen-in-Parliament constituted the highest court in the realm for most purposes, but the Privy Council had jurisdiction in some cases (for instance, appeals from ecclesiastical courts). The jurisdiction of Parliament arose from the ancient custom of petitioning the Houses to redress grievances and to do justice. The House of Commons ceased considering petitions to reverse the judgements of lower courts in 1399, effectively leaving the House of Lords as the court of last resort. In modern times, the judicial functions of the House of Lords were performed not by the whole House, but by a group of "Lords of Appeal in Ordinary" (judges granted life peerage dignities under the Appellate Jurisdiction Act 1876 by the Sovereign) and by "Lords of Appeal" (other peers with experience in the judiciary). However, under the Constitutional Reform Act 2005, these judicial functions were transferred to the newly created Supreme Court in 2009, and the Lords of Appeal in Ordinary became the first Justices of the Court. Peers who hold high judicial office are no longer allowed to vote or speak in the Lords until they retire as Justices.

In the late 19th century, Acts allowed for the appointment of *Scottish Lords of Appeal in Ordinary* and ended appeal in Scottish criminal matters to the House of Lords, so that the High Court of Justiciary became the highest criminal court in Scotland. There is an argument that the provisions of Article XIX of the Union with England Act 1707 prevent any Court outside Scotland from hearing any appeal in criminal cases: *"And that the said Courts or any other of the like nature after the Unions shall have no power to Cognosce Review or Alter the Acts or Sentences of the Judicatures within Scotland or stop the Execution of the same."* Nowadays the House of Lords legislative committee usually has a minimum of two Scottish Judges to ensure that some experience of Scots law is brought to bear on Scottish appeals in civil cases, from the Court of Session.

Certain other judicial functions have historically been performed by the House of Lords. Until 1948, it was the body in which peers had to be tried for felonies or high treason; now, they are tried by normal juries. When the House of Commons impeaches an individual, the trial takes place in the House of Lords. Impeachments are now rare; the last one occurred in 1806. In 2006, a number of MPs attempted to revive the custom, having signed a motion for the impeachment of Tony Blair, but this was unsuccessful.

Relationship with the Government

The British Government is answerable to the House of Commons. However, neither the Prime Minister nor members of the Government are elected by the House of Commons. Instead, the Queen requests the person most likely to command the support of a majority in the House, normally the leader of the largest party in the House of Commons, to form a government. So that they may be accountable to the Lower House, the Prime Minister and most members of the Cabinet are, by convention, members of the House of Commons. The last Prime Minister to be a member of the House of Lords was Alec Douglas-Home, 14th Earl of Home, who became Prime Minister in 1963. To adhere to the convention under which he was responsible to the Lower House, he disclaimed his peerage and procured election to the House of Commons within days of becoming Prime Minister.

Governments have a tendency to dominate the legislative functions of Parliament, by using their in-built majority in the House of Commons, and sometimes using their patronage power to appoint supportive peers in the Lords. In practice, governments can pass any legislation (within reason) in the Commons they wish, unless there is major dissent by MPs in the governing party. But even in these situations, it is highly unlikely a bill will be defeated, though dissenting MPs may be able to extract concessions from the government. In 1976, Lord Hailsham created a now widely used name for this behaviour, in an academic paper called "elective dictatorship".

Parliament controls the executive by passing or rejecting its Bills and by forcing Ministers of the Crown to answer for their actions, either at "Question Time" or during meetings of the parliamentary committees. In both cases, Ministers are asked questions by members of their Houses, and are obliged to answer.

Although the House of Lords may scrutinise the executive through Question Time and through its committees, it cannot bring down the Government. A ministry must always retain the confidence and support of the House of Commons. The Lower House may indicate its lack of support by rejecting a Motion of Confidence or by passing a Motion of No Confidence. Confidence Motions are generally originated by the Government in order to reinforce its support in the House, whilst No Confidence Motions are introduced by the Opposition. The motions sometimes take the form "That this House has [no] confidence in Her Majesty's Government" but several other varieties, many referring to specific policies supported or opposed by Parliament, are used. For instance, a Confidence Motion of 1992 used the form, "That this House expresses the support for the economic policy of Her Majesty's Government." Such a motion may theoretically be introduced in the House of Lords, but, as the Government need not enjoy the confidence of that House, would not be of the same effect as a similar motion in the House of Commons; the only modern instance of such an occurrence involves the 'No Confidence' motion that was introduced in 1993 and subsequently defeated.

Many votes are considered votes of confidence, although not including the language mentioned above. Important bills that form part of the Government's agenda (as stated in the Speech from the Throne) are generally considered matters of confidence. The defeat of such a bill by the House of Commons indicates that a Government no longer has the confidence of that House. The same effect is achieved if the House of Commons "withdraws Supply", that is, rejects the budget.

Where a Government has lost the confidence of the House of Commons, the Prime Minister is obliged either to resign, or seek the dissolution of Parliament and a new general election. Where a Prime Minister has ceased to retain a majority in that vote and requests a dissolution, the Sovereign can in theory reject his request, forcing his resignation and allowing the Leader of the Opposition to be asked to form a new government. This power is used extremely rarely. The conditions that should be met to allow such a refusal are known as the Lascelles Principles. These conditions and principles are merely informal conventions; it is possible, though highly improbable, for the Sovereign to refuse dissolution for no reason at all.

In practice, the House of Commons' scrutiny of the Government is very weak. Since the first-past-the-post electoral system is employed in elections, the governing party tends to enjoy a large majority in the Commons; there is often limited need to compromise with other parties. Modern British political parties are so tightly organised that they leave relatively little room for free action by their MPs. In many cases, MPs may be expelled from their parties for voting against the instructions of party leaders. During the 20th century, the Government has lost confidence issues only three times—twice in 1924, and once in 1979.

Parliamentary Questions

In the United Kingdom, question time in the House of Commons lasts for an hour each day from Monday to Thursday (2:30 to 3:30pm on Mondays, 11:30am to 12:30pm on Tuesdays and Wednesdays, and 9:30 to 10:30am on Thursdays). Each Government department has its place in a rota which repeats every five weeks. The exception to this sequence are the Business Questions (Questions to the Leader of House of Commons), in which questions are answered each Thursday about the business of the House the following week. Also, Questions to the Prime Minister takes place each Wednesday from noon to 12:30pm.

In addition to government departments, there are also questions to the Church commissioners.[] Additionally, each Member of Parliament is entitled to table questions for written answer. Written questions are addressed to the Ministerial head of a government department, usually a Secretary of State, but they are often answered by a Minister of State or Parliamentary Under Secretary of State. Written Questions are submitted to the Clerks of the Table Office, either on paper or electronically, and answers are recorded in *The Official Report (Hansard)* so as to be widely available and accessible.[]

In the House of Lords, a half hour is set aside each afternoon at the start of the day's proceedings for Lords' oral questions. A peer submits a question in advance, which then appears on the Order Paper for the day's proceedings.[] The Lord shall say: "*My Lords, I beg leave to ask the Question standing in my name on the Order Paper*". The Minister responsible then answers the question. The Lord is then allowed to ask a supplementary question and other peers ask further questions on the theme of the original put down on the order paper. (For instance, if the question regards immigration, Lords can ask the Minister any question related to immigration during the allowed period).[]

Sovereignty

Parliament Buildings, Stormont, Northern Ireland is home to the Northern Ireland Assembly.

Several different views have been taken of Parliament's sovereignty. According to the jurist Sir William Blackstone, "It has sovereign and uncontrollable authority in making, confirming, enlarging, restraining, abrogating, repealing, reviving, and expounding of laws, concerning matters of all possible denominations, ecclesiastical, or temporal, civil, military, maritime, or criminal ... it can, in short, do every thing that is not naturally impossible."

A different view has been taken by the Scottish judge Lord Cooper of Culross. When he decided the 1953 case of *MacCormick v. Lord Advocate* as Lord President of the Court of Session, he stated, "The principle of unlimited sovereignty of Parliament is a distinctively English principle and has no counterpart in Scottish constitutional law." He continued, "Considering that the Union legislation extinguished the Parliaments of Scotland and England and replaced them by a new Parliament, I have difficulty in seeing why the new Parliament of Great Britain must inherit all the peculiar characteristics of the English Parliament but none of the Scottish." Nevertheless, he did not give a conclusive opinion on the subject.

Thus, the question of Parliamentary sovereignty appears to remain unresolved. Parliament has not passed any Act defining its own sovereignty. A related possible limitation on Parliament relates to the Scottish legal system and Presbyterian faith, preservation of which were Scottish preconditions to the creation of the unified Parliament. Since the Parliament of the United Kingdom was set up in reliance on these promises, it may be that it has no power to make laws that break them.

Parliament's power has often been eroded by its own Acts. Acts passed in 1921 and 1925 granted the Church of Scotland complete independence in ecclesiastical matters. More recently, its power has been restricted by membership of the European Union, which has the power to make laws enforceable in each member state. In the Factortame case, the European Court of Justice ruled that British courts could have powers to overturn British legislation contravening European law.

Parliament has also created national devolved parliaments and assemblies with differing degrees of legislative authority in Scotland, Wales and Northern Ireland. Parliament still has the power over areas for which responsibility lies with the devolved institutions, but would gain the agreement of those institutions to act on their behalf. Similarly, it has granted the power to make regulations to Ministers of the Crown, and the power to enact religious legislation to the General Synod of the Church of England. (Measures of the General Synod and, in some cases proposed statutory instruments made by ministers, must be approved by both Houses before they become law.)

In every case aforementioned, authority has been conceded by Act of Parliament and may be taken back in the same manner. It is entirely within the authority of Parliament, for example, to abolish the devolved governments in Scotland, Wales and Northern Ireland or to leave the EU. However, Parliament also revoked its legislative competence over Australia and Canada with the Australia and Canada Acts: although the Parliament of the United Kingdom could pass an Act reversing its action, it would not take effect in Australia or Canada as the competence of the **Imperial Parliament** is no longer recognised there in law.

One well-recognised exception to Parliament's power involves binding future Parliaments. No Act of Parliament may be made secure from amendment or repeal by a future Parliament. For example, although the Act of Union 1800 states that the Kingdoms of Great Britain and Ireland are to be united "forever", Parliament permitted southern Ireland to leave the United Kingdom in 1922.

Privileges

Each House of Parliament possesses and guards various ancient privileges. The House of Lords relies on inherent right. In the case of the House of Commons, the Speaker goes to the Lords' Chamber at the beginning of each new Parliament and requests representatives of the Sovereign to confirm the Lower House's "undoubted" privileges and rights. The ceremony observed by the House of Commons dates to the reign of King Henry VIII. Each House is the guardian of its privileges, and may punish breaches thereof. The extent of parliamentary privilege is based on law and custom. Sir William Blackstone states that these privileges are "very large and indefinite", and cannot be defined except by the Houses of Parliament themselves.

The foremost privilege claimed by both Houses is that of freedom of speech in debate; nothing said in either House may be questioned in any court or other institution outside Parliament. Another privilege claimed is that of freedom from arrest; at one time this was held to apply for any arrest except for high treason, felony or breach of the peace but it now excludes any arrest on criminal charges; it applies during a session of Parliament, and 40 days before or after such a session.[14] Members of both Houses are no longer privileged from service on juries.[15]

Both Houses possess the power to punish breaches of their privilege. Contempt of Parliament—for example, disobedience of a subpoena issued by a committee—may also be punished. The House of Lords may imprison an individual for any fixed period of time, but an individual imprisoned by the House of Commons is set free upon prorogation.[16] The punishments imposed by either House may not be challenged in any court, and the Human Rights Act does not apply.[17]

Emblem

The quasi-official emblem of the Houses of Parliament is a crowned portcullis. The portcullis was originally the badge of various English noble families from the 14th century. It went on to be adopted by the kings of the Tudor dynasty in the 16th century, under whom the Palace of Westminster became the regular meeting place of Parliament. The crown was added to make the badge a specifically royal symbol.

The Crowned Portcullis of Parliament

The portcullis probably first came to be associated with the Palace of Westminster through its use as decoration in the rebuilding of the Palace after the fire of 1512. However, at the time it was only one of many symbols. The widespread use of the portcullis throughout the Palace dates from the 19th century, when Charles Barry and Augustus Pugin used it extensively as a decorative feature in their designs for the new Palace built following the disastrous 1834 fire.

The crowned portcullis came to be accepted during the 20th century as the emblem of both houses of parliament. This was simply a result of custom and usage rather than a specific decision. The emblem now appears on official stationery, publications and papers, and is stamped on various items in use in the Palace of Westminster, such as cutlery, silverware and china..[18] various shades of red and green are used for visual identification of the House of Lords and the House of Commons

See also

- History of democracy
- History of Parliament
- Parliamentary agents
- Parliamentary Brief
- Parliamentary records of the United Kingdom
- Records of members of parliament of the United Kingdom
- List of Acts of the Parliament of the United Kingdom
- List of British Governments
- List of British ministries
- List of Parliamentary constituencies in the United Kingdom
- List of Parliaments of the United Kingdom
- Westminster system
- TheyWorkForYou

Lists of MPs elected:

- List of MPs elected in the United Kingdom general election, 1966
- List of MPs elected in the United Kingdom general election, 1970
- MPs elected in the United Kingdom general election, February 1974
- MPs elected in the United Kingdom general election, October 1974
- List of MPs elected in the United Kingdom general election, 1979
- List of MPs elected in the United Kingdom general election, 1983
- List of MPs elected in the United Kingdom general election, 1987
- List of MPs elected in the United Kingdom general election, 1992
- List of MPs elected in the United Kingdom general election, 1997
- List of MPs elected in the United Kingdom general election, 2001
- List of MPs elected in the United Kingdom general election, 2005
- List of MPs elected in the United Kingdom general election, 2010

Notes

[1] Section 2 of the Royal and Parliamentary Titles Act 1927 (http://www.statutelaw.gov.uk/content.aspx?LegType=All+Primary&PageNumber=84&NavFrom=2&parentActiveTextDocId=1080244&ActiveTextDocId=1080244&filesize=4238) (17 Geo. V c. 4)

[4] Direct.gov.uk (http://www.direct.gov.uk/en/Governmentcitizensandrights/UKgovernment/Parliament/DG_073604)

[17] Human Rights Act 1998, section 6(3).

[18] The Portcullis (factsheet) (http://www.parliament.uk/documents/documents/upload/2009-HCIO-Factsheet-Portcullis.pdf), House of Commons Information Office, November 2007

References

- "Parliament". (1911). *Encyclopædia Britannica,* 11th ed. London: Cambridge University Press.
- E. A. Wasson, *Born to Rule: British Political Elites* (Stroud, 2000).

External links

- United Kingdom Parliament (http://www.parliament.uk/). Official website.
- Public Policy Hub - Parliament and law making (http://sshls-dev.port.ac.uk/hub/public-policy/structures/parliament-and-law-making/)

Legislature

Legislature
This series is part of the Politics series

• Legislature
• Legislatures by country
• Parliament
  • Member of Parliament
  • Parliamentary group
    • Parliamentary group leader
    • Frontbench
• Congress
  • Congressperson
• International parliament
• Unicameralism
• Multicameralism
  • Bicameralism
  • Tricameralism (historical)
  • Tetracameralism (historical)
• Chambers of parliament
  • Upper house (Senate)
  • Lower house
• Parliamentary system
• City council
  • Councillor

Politics Portal · [1]

A **legislature** is a kind of deliberative assembly with the power to pass, amend, and repeal laws.[2] The law created by a legislature is called legislation or statutory law. In addition to enacting laws, legislatures usually have exclusive authority to raise or lower taxes and adopt the budget and other money bills. Legislatures are known by many names, the most common being parliament and congress, although these terms also have more specific meanings.

In parliamentary systems of government, the legislature is formally supreme and appoints a member from its house as the prime minister which acts as the executive.[3] In a presidential system, according to the separation of powers doctrine, the legislature is considered an independent and coequal branch of government along with both the judiciary and the executive.[4]

The primary components of a legislature are one or more *chambers* or *houses*: assemblies that can debate and vote upon bills. A legislature with only one house is called unicameral. A bicameral legislature possesses two separate chambers, usually described as an upper house and a lower house, which often differ in duties, powers, and the methods used for the selection of members. Much rarer have been tricameral legislatures; the Massachusetts Governor's Council still exists, but the most recent national example existed in the waning years of caucasian-minority rule in South Africa.

In most parliamentary systems, the lower house is the more powerful house while the upper house is merely a chamber of advice or review. However, in presidential systems, the powers of the two houses are often similar or equal. In federations, it is typical for the upper house to represent the component states; the same applies to the supranational legislature of the European Union. For this purpose, the upper house may either contain the delegates of state governments, as is the case in the European Union and in Germany and was the case in the United States before 1913, or be elected according to a formula that grants equal representation to states with smaller populations, as is the case in Australia and the contemporary United States.

Because members of legislatures usually sit together in a specific room to deliberate, seats in that room may be assigned exclusively to members of the legislature. In parliamentary language, the term *seat* is sometimes used to mean that someone is a member of a legislature. For example, saying that a legislature has 100 "seats" means that there are 100 members of the legislature, and saying that someone is "contesting a seat" means they are trying to get elected as a member of the legislature. By extension, the term *seat* is often used in less formal contexts to refer to an electoral district itself, as for example in the phrases "safe seat" and "marginal seat".

See also

- Legislative Council
- List of legislatures by country
- Parliamentary system

Notes and references

[1] http://en.wikipedia.org/wiki/Template:Legislature

Parliament

A **parliament** is a legislature whose power and function are similar to those dictated by the Westminster system of the United Kingdom. More generally, "parliament" may simply refer to a democratic government's legislature. The term is derived from the French *parlement*, the action of *parler* (to speak): a *parlement* is a discussion. The term came to mean a meeting at which such a discussion took place. It acquired its modern meaning as it came to be used for the body of people (in an institutional sense) who would meet to discuss matters of state.[]

The chamber of the House of Commons of the British Parliament in the City of Westminster, London.

Generally, a parliament has three functions: representation, legislation and parliamentary control (i.e., hearings, inquiries).

The House of Representatives Chamber of the Parliament of Australia in Canberra.

Origins

Various bodies appeared under different names in many medieval European kingdoms to act as advisory councils for the monarchs and to represent barons, commoners and the church. The use of the *term* 'parliament' to designate such a body first occurred in England in 1236. Previously, this group of the king's closest advisors had been called the "council". After agreeing to the principle of “common consent” in the Magna Carta, King John had to increase the size of this group of advisors and include more commoners. He then had to submit his requests for increased taxation to this newly expanded group. Two distinct groups emerged among the commoners: the landed gentry, and the rich merchants and lawyers.

The word “parliament” comes from the French “parler”, which means “to talk” or “to discuss”. English parliamentary procedure, such as Jefferson's Manual of Parliamentary Procedure, developed not to facilitate talk, but to facilitate decision-making. Although the British model of parliament, known as the Westminster Model, is held up as the “Mother of all Parliaments”, it is unique in that it developed over time from tradition, as opposed to being democratically enacted by way of a constitution.[]

Parliament government

Legislatures called parliaments operate under a parliamentary system of government in which the executive is constitutionally answerable to the parliament. Parliaments usually consist of *chambers* or *houses*, and are usually either bicameral or unicameral although more complex models exist, or have existed (*see Tricameralism*).

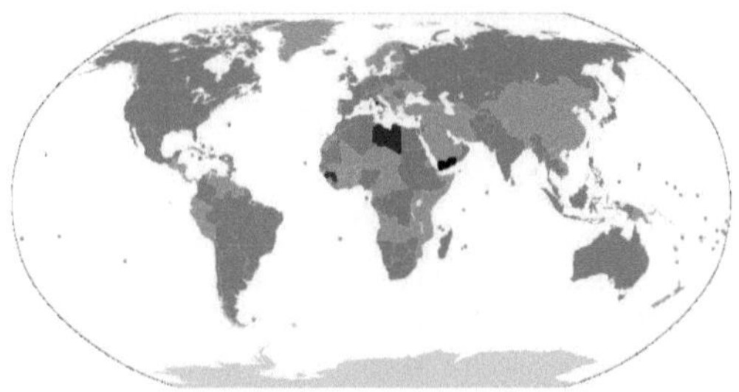

Nations with bicameral legislatures. Nations with unicameral legislatures. No legislature.

A nation's prime minister (PM) is almost always the leader of the majority party in the lower house of parliament, but only holds his or her office as long as the "confidence of the house" is maintained. If members of the lower house lose faith in the leader for whatever reason, they can call a vote of no confidence and force the PM to resign.

This can be particularly dangerous to a government when the distribution of seats among different parties is relatively even, in which case a new election is often called shortly thereafter. However, in case of general discontent with the head of government, his replacement can be made very smoothly without all the complications that it represents in the case of a presidential system.

The parliamentary system can be contrasted with a presidential system, on the model of the United States' congressional system, which operate under a stricter separation of powers whereby the executive does not form part of, nor is appointed by, the parliamentary or legislative body. In such a system, congresses do not select or dismiss heads of governments, and governments cannot request an early dissolution as may be the case for parliaments. Some states have a semi-presidential system which falls between parliamentary and congressional systems, and combines a powerful head of state (president) with a head of government (PM) responsible to parliament.

Proto-parliamentarian institutions

See History of Parliamentarism

Since ancient times, when societies were tribal, there were councils or a headman whose decisions were assessed by village elders. This is called tribalism.[1] Some scholars suggest that in ancient Mesopotamia there was a primitive democratic government where the kings were assessed by council.[2] The same has been said about ancient India, where some form of deliberative assemblies existed, and therefore there was some form of democracy.[3] However, these claims are not accepted by most scholars, who see these forms of government as oligarchies.[4] [5] [6] [7] [8]

Ancient Athens was the cradle of democracy.[9] The Athenian assembly (ἐκκλησία ekklesia) was the most important institution, and every citizen could take part in the discussions. However, Athenian democracy was not representative, but rather direct, and therefore the ekklesia was different from the parliamentary system.

The Roman republic had legislative assemblies, who had the final say regarding the election of magistrates, the enactment of new statutes, the carrying out of capital punishment, the declaration of war and peace, and the creation (or dissolution) of alliances.[10] The Roman Senate controlled money, administration, and the details of foreign policy.[11]

Some Muslim scholars argue that the Islamic shura (a method of taking decisions in Islamic societies) is analogous to the parliament.[12] However, many others disagree, highlighting some fundamental differences between the shura system and the parliamentary system.[13] [14] [15]

In Anglo-Saxon England, the Witenagamot was an important political institution. The name derives from the Old English pitena ȝemōt, or witena gemōt, for "meeting of wise men". The first recorded act of a witenagemot was the law code issued by King Æthelberht of Kent ca. 600, the earliest document which survives in sustained Old English prose; however, the witan was certainly in existence long before this time.[16] The Witan, along with the folkmoots(local assemblies), is an important ancestor of the modern English parliament.[17]

England

England has long had a tradition of a body of men who would assist and advise the King on important matters. Under the Anglo-Saxon Kings, there was an advisory council, the Witenagemot ("meeting of wise men"). As part of the Norman Conquest of England, the new King, William I, did away with the Witenagemot, replacing it with a Curia Regis ("King's Council"). Membership of the Curia was largely restricted to the tenants in chief, the few nobles who "rented" great estates directly from the King, along with certain senior ecclesiastics.

Most historians date the emergence of a parliament with some degree of power to which the throne had to defer no later than the rule of Edward I. (Kaeuper, Richard W., War Justice and Public Order: England and France in the Later Middle Ages, Oxford U. Press, 1988.) Like previous kings, Edward called leading nobles and church leaders to discuss government matters, especially finance. A meeting in 1295 became known as the Model Parliament because it set the pattern for later Parliaments. The significant difference between the Model Parliament and the earlier Curia Regis was the addition of the Commons, that is, elected representatives of rural landowners and of townsmen. In 1307, Edward I agreed not to collect certain taxes without consent of the realm. He also enlarged the court system.

William of Normandy brought to England the feudal system of his native Normandy, and sought the advice of the curia regis, before making laws. This body is the origin from which the Parliament, the higher courts of law, the Privy Council and Cabinet have sprung. Of these, the legislature is formally the High Court of Parliament; judges sit in the Supreme Court of Judicature; and only the executive government is no longer conducted in a royal court.

The tenants-in-chief often struggled with their spiritual counterparts and with the King for power. In 1215, they secured from John the Magna Carta, which established that the King may not levy or collect any taxes (except the feudal taxes to which they were hitherto accustomed), save with the consent of a council. It was also established that the most important tenants-in-chief and ecclesiastics be summoned to the council by personal writs from the Sovereign, and that all others be summoned to the council by general writs from the sheriffs of their counties. Modern government has its origins in the Curia Regis; parliament descends from the Great Council later known as the *parliamentum* established by Magna Carta.

The English Parliaments during the reign of King Henry III in the 13th century incorporated elected representation from shires and towns, and is considered the forerunner of the modern parliament.[18] In 1265, Simon de Montfort, 6th Earl of Leicester, who was in rebellion against Henry III, summoned a parliament of his supporters without royal authorisation. The archbishops, bishops, abbots, earls and barons were summoned, as were two knights from each shire and two burgesses from each borough. Knights had been summoned to previous councils, but the representation of the boroughs was unprecedented. De Montfort's scheme of representation and election was formally adopted by Edward I in the so-called "Model Parliament" of 1295. At first, each estate debated independently; by the reign of Edward III, however, Parliament had been separated into two Houses and was recognisably assuming its modern form.

Parliament under Henry VIII and Edward VI

The purpose and structure of parliament in Tudor England underwent a significant transformation under the reign of Henry VIII. Originally its methods were primarily medieval and the monarch still had inarguable dominion over the decisions. According to Elton, it was Cromwell who then initiated the beginnings of change within parliament.

The Reformation Acts gave parliament unlimited power over the country, and authority over every matter, be it social, economic, political or even religious ; it legalised the Reformation, officially and indisputably. The King had to rule through the council, not over it, and there had to be mutual agreement when creating or passing laws, changing religions or adjusting taxes. The monarch no longer had sole control over the country. For instance, during the later years of Mary, the parliament originally rejected Mary's intent to revive Catholicism in the realm, and even later, denied Elizabeth her request for marriage . If parliament had had this power before Cromwell, during Wolsey's reign as Secretary, the reformation might never have happened as the king would have had to gain the consent of all parliament members before so drastically changing the country's religious laws .

The effectiveness of parliament considerably increased after Cromwell's adjustments. It gave the country an unprecedented stability when dealing with dynastic complications, such as a minor king or the lack of a suitable heir. When an acceptable monarch was not available, the changes in government meant that the country could still run efficiently through the parliament, without having to succumb to civil war. Management and organisation was also improved and parliamentary procedure was documented, statutes printed. The fact that the monarch was suddenly dependent on another political body meant that decisions were more thoroughly considered and the rash whims of Henry VIII were trivialised and reduced. He could not establish supremacy by proclamation; he needed the parliament to enforce statute, to add felonies and treasons. One of the main liberties of parliament was its freedom of speech; Henry allowed anything to be spoken openly within parliament and the speakers were not allowed to be arrested, a fact which they exploited incessantly. Despite this fact however, parliament held very little objection to the desires of the monarch, and under Henry and Edward's reign it complied willingly to the majority of the Kings' decisions.

As Williams described it, "King and parliament were not separate entities, but a single body, of which the monarch was the senior partner and the Lords and the Commons the lesser, but still essential, members."

The Parliament of England met until the Acts of Union merged the Parliament of Scotland and the Parliament of England, creating the new Parliament of Great Britain in 1707.

France

Originally, there was only the Parliament of Paris, born out of the Curia Regis in 1307, and located inside the medieval royal palace, now the Paris Hall of Justice. The jurisdiction of the *Parliament* of Paris covered the entire kingdom. In the thirteenth century, judicial functions were added. In 1443, following the turmoil of the Hundred Years' War, King Charles VII of France granted Languedoc its own *parliament* by establishing the *Parliament* of Toulouse, the first *parliament* outside of Paris, whose jurisdiction extended over the most part of southern France. From 1443 until the French Revolution several other *parliaments* were created in some provinces of France (Grenoble, Bordeaux).

All the *parliaments* could issue regulatory decrees for the application of royal edicts or of customary practices; they could also refuse to register laws that they judged contrary to fundamental law or simply as being untimely. Parliamentary power in France was suppressed more so than in England as a result of absolutism, and parliaments were eventually overshadowed by the larger Estates General, up until the French Revolution, when the National Assembly became the lower house of France's bicameral legislature.

Scotland

The debating chamber of the reconvened Scottish Parliament from the public gallery.

From the 10th century the Kingdom of Alba was ruled by chiefs (*toisechs*) and subkings (*mormaers*) under the suzerainty, real or nominal, of a High King. Popular assemblies, as in Ireland, were involved in law-making, and sometimes in king-making, although the introduction of tanistry—naming a successor in the lifetime of a king—made the second less than common. These early assemblies cannot be considered "parliaments" in the later sense of the word, and were entirely separate from the later, Norman-influenced, institution.

The Parliament of Scotland evolved during the Middle Ages from the King's Council of Bishops and Earls. The unicameral parliament is first found on record, referred to as a *colloquium*, in 1235 at Kirkliston (a village now in Edinburgh).

By the early fourteenth century the attendance of knights and freeholders had become important, and from 1326 burgh commissioners attended. Consisting of the Three Estates; of clerics, lay tenants-in-chief and burgh commissioners sitting in a single chamber, the Scottish parliament acquired significant powers over particular issues. Most obviously it was needed for consent for taxation (although taxation was only raised irregularly in Scotland in the medieval period), but it also had a strong influence over justice, foreign policy, war, and all manner of other legislation, whether political, ecclesiastical, social or economic. Parliamentary business was also carried out by "sister" institutions, before c. 1500 by General Council and thereafter by the Convention of Estates. These could carry out much business also dealt with by Parliament – taxation, legislation and policy-making – but lacked the ultimate authority of a full parliament.

The parliament, which is also referred to as the Estates of Scotland, the Three Estates, the Scots Parliament or the auld Scots Parliament (Eng: *old*), met until the Acts of Union merged the Parliament of Scotland and the Parliament of England, creating the new Parliament of Great Britain in 1707.

Following the Scottish devolution referendum, 1997, and the passing of the Scotland Act 1998 by the Parliament of the United Kingdom, the Scottish Parliament was reconvened on 1 July 1999, although with much more limited powers than its 18th century predecessor. The parliament has sat since 2004 at its newly constructed Scottish Parliament Building in Edinburgh, situated at the foot of the Royal Mile, next to the royal palace of Holyroodhouse.

Nordic and Germanic development

Iceland's parliament House, at Austurvöllur in Reykjavík, built in 1880–1881. Home of one of the oldest still-acting parliaments in the world.

A *thing* or *ting* (Old Norse and Icelandic: *þing*; other modern Scandinavian: *ting*, *ding* in Dutch) was the governing assembly in Germanic societies, made up of the free men of the community and presided by lawspeakers. Today the term lives on in the official names of national legislatures, political and judicial institutions in the North-Germanic countries. In the Yorkshire and former Danelaw areas of England, which were subject to much Norse invasion and settlement, the wapentake was another name for the same institution.

The thing was the assembly of the free men of a country, province or a hundred *(hundare/härad/herred)*. There were consequently, hierarchies of things, so that the local things were represented at the thing for a larger area, for a province or land. At the thing, disputes were solved and political decisions were made. The place for the thing was often also the place for public religious rites and for commerce.

The thing met at regular intervals, legislated, elected chieftains and kings, and judged according to the law, which was memorised and recited by the "law speaker" (the judge).

Later national diets with chambers for different estates developed, e.g. in Sweden and in Finland (which was part of Sweden until 1809), each with a House of Knights for the nobility. In both these countries, the national parliaments are now called riksdag (in Finland also *eduskunta*), a word used since the Middle Ages and equivalent of the German word Reichstag.

Poland

Chamber of the Sejm showing the hemicycle seating pattern.

According to the *Chronicles* of Gallus Anonymus, the first legendary Polish ruler, Siemowit, who began the Piast Dynasty, was chosen by a *wiec*. The *veche* (Russian: вече, Polish: *wiec*) was a popular assembly in medieval Slavic countries, and in late medieval period, a parliament. The idea of the *wiec* led in 1182 to the development of the Polish parliament, the *Sejm*.

The term "sejm" comes from an old Polish expression denoting a meeting of the populace. The power of early sejms grew between 1146–1295, when the power of individual rulers waned and various councils and wiece grew stronger. The history of the national Sejm dates back to 1182. Since the 14th century irregular sejms (described in various Latin sources as *contentio generalis, conventio magna, conventio solemna, parlamentum, parlamentum generale, dieta* or Polish *sejm walny*) have been called by Polish kings. From 1374, the king had to receive sejm permission to raise taxes. The General Sejm (Polish *Sejm Generalny* or *Sejm Walny*), first convoked by the king John I Olbracht in 1493 near Piotrków, evolved from earlier regional and provincial meetings (*sejmiks*). It followed most closely the *sejmik generally*, which arose from the 1454 Nieszawa Statutes, granted to the szlachta (nobles) by King Casimir IV the Jagiellonian. From 1493 forward, indirect elections were repeated every two years. With the development of the unique Polish Golden Liberty the Sejm's powers increased.

The Commonwealth's general parliament consisted of three estates: the King of Poland (who also acted as the Grand Duke of Lithuania, Russia/Ruthenia, Prussia, Mazovia, etc.), the Senat (consisting of Ministers, Palatines, Castellans and Bishops) and the Chamber of Envoys—circa 170 nobles (szlachta) acting on behalf of their Lands and sent by Land Parliaments. Also representatives of selected cities but without any voting powers. Since 1573 at a royal election all peers of the Commonwealth could participate in the Parliament and become the King's electors.

Ukraine

Cossack Rada was the legislative body of a military republic of cossacks that grew rapidly in the 15th century from serfs fleeing the more controlled parts of the Polish Lithuanian Commonwealth. The republic did not regard social origin/nobility and accepted all people who declared to be Orthodox Christians.

Russia

The name of the parliament of Russian Federation is the Federal Assembly of Russia. The term for its lower house, Duma (which is better known than the Federal Assembly itself, and is often mistaken for the entirety of the parliament) comes from the Russian word *думать* (*dumat*), "to think". The **Boyar Duma** was an advisory council to the grand princes and tsars of Muscovy. The Duma was discontinued by Peter the Great, who transferred its functions to the Governing Senate in 1711.

Novgorod and Pskov

The *veche* was the highest legislature and judicial authority in the republic of Novgorod until 1478. In its sister state, Pskov, a separate veche operated until 1510.

Since the Novgorod revolution of 1137 ousted the ruling grand prince, the veche became the supreme state authority. After the reforms of 1410, the veche was restructured on a model similar to that of Venice, becoming the Commons chamber of the parliament. An upper Senate-like Council of Lords was also created, with title membership for all former city magistrates. Some sources indicate that veche membership may have became full-time, and parliament deputies were now called *vechniks*. It is recounted that the Novgorod assembly could be summoned by anyone who rung the veche bell, although it is more likely that the common procedure was more complex. This bell was a symbol of republican sovereignty and independence. The whole population of the city—boyars, merchants, and common citizens—then gathered at Yaroslav's Court. Separate assemblies could be held in the districts of Novgorod. In Pskov the veche assembled in the court of the Trinity cathedral.

Spain

Although there are documented councils held in 873, 1020, 1050 and 1063, there was no representation of commoners. What is considered to be the first Spanish parliament (with the presence of commoners), the Cortes, was held in the Kingdom of León in 1188.[19] [20] [21] Prelates, nobles and commoners met separately in the three estates of the Cortes. In this meeting new laws were approved to protect commoners against the arbitrarities of nobles, prelates and the king. This important set of laws is known as the *Carta Magna Leonesa*.

Congreso de los Diputados, lower house of the Spanish Parliament

Following this event, new Cortes would appear in the other different territories that would make up Spain: Catalonia in 1218, the Kingdom of Castile in 1250, Kingdom of Aragon in 1274, Kingdom of Valencia in 1283 and Kingdom of Navarre in 1300.

After the union of the Kingdoms of Leon and Castile under the Crown of Castile, their Cortes were united as well in 1258. The Castilian Cortes had representatives from Burgos, Toledo, León, Seville, Córdoba, Murcia, Jaén, Zamora, Segovia, Ávila, Salamanca, Cuenca, Toro, Valladolid, Soria, Madrid, Guadalajara and Granada (after 1492). The Cortes' assent was required to pass new taxes, and could also advise the king on other matters. The comunero rebels intended a stronger role for the Cortes, but were defeated by the forces of Habsburg Emperor Charles V in 1521. The Cortes maintained some power, however, though it became more of a consultative entity. However, by the time of King Philip II, Charles's son, the Castilian Cortes had come under functionally complete royal control, with its delegates dependent on the Crown for their income.[22]

The Cortes of the Crown of Aragon kingdoms retained their power to control the king's spending with regard to the finances of those kingdoms. But after the War of the Spanish Succession and the arrival of another royal house – the Bourbons – in 1714 with Philip V, their Cortes were suppressed (as were those of Aragon and Valencia in 1707, Catalonia and Balearic islands in 1714).

The Roman Catholic Church

"Conciliarism" or the "conciliar movement", was a reform movement in the 14th and 15th century Roman Catholic Church which held that final authority in spiritual matters resided with the Roman Church as corporation of Christians, embodied by a general church council, not with the pope. In effect, the movement sought – ultimately, in vain – to create an All-Catholic Parliament. Its struggle with the Papacy had many points in common with the struggle of parliaments in specific countries against the authority of Kings and other secular rulers.

Parliaments of the United Kingdom

The British Parliament is often referred to as the *Mother of Parliaments* (in fact a misquotation of John Bright, who remarked in 1865 that "England is the Mother of Parliaments") because the British Parliament has been the model for most other parliamentary systems, and its Acts have created many other parliaments. Many nations with parliaments have to some degree emulated the British "three-tier" model. Most countries in Europe and the Commonwealth have similarly organised parliaments with a largely ceremonial head of state who formally opens and closes parliament, a large elected lower house and a smaller, upper house.

The British Houses of Parliament, London

The Parliament of Great Britain was formed in 1707 by the Acts of Union that replaced the former parliaments of England and Scotland. A further union in 1801 united the Parliament of Great Britain and the Parliament of Ireland into a Parliament of the United Kingdom.

In the United Kingdom, Parliament consists of the House of Commons, the House of Lords, and the Monarch. The House of Commons is composed of 650 members who are directly elected by British citizens to represent single-member constituencies. The leader of a Party that wins more than half the seats or less than half but can count on support of smaller parties to achieve enough support to pass law is invited by the Queen to form a government. The House of Lords is a body of long-serving, unelected members: 92 of whom inherit their titles (and of whom 90 are elected internally by members of the House to lifetime seats), 26 bishops while they remain in office, and 588 of whom have been appointed to lifetime seats.

Legislation can originate from either the Lords or the Commons. It is voted on in several distinct stages, called readings, in each house. First reading is merely a formality. Second reading is where the bill as a whole is considered. Third reading is detailed consideration of clauses of the bill.

In addition to the three readings a bill also goes through a committee stage where it is considered in great detail. Once the bill has been passed by one house it goes to the other and essentially repeats the process. If after the two sets of readings there are disagreements between the versions that the two houses passed it is returned to the first house for consideration of the amendments made by the second. If it passes through the amendment stage Royal Assent is granted and the bill becomes law as an Act of Parliament.

The House of Lords is the less powerful of the two houses as a result of the Parliament Acts 1911 and 1949. These Acts removed the veto power of the Lords over a great deal of legislation. If a bill is certified by the Speaker of the House of Commons as a money bill (i.e. acts raising taxes and similar) then the Lords can only block it for a month. If an ordinary bill originates in the Commons the Lords can only block it for a maximum of one session of Parliament. The exceptions to this rule are things like bills to prolong the life of a Parliament beyond five years.

In addition to functioning as the second chamber of Parliament, the House of Lords was also the final court of appeal for much of the law of the United Kingdom—a combination of judicial and legislative function that recalls its origin in the Curia Regis. This changed in October 2009 when the Supreme Court of the United Kingdom opened and acquired the former jurisdiction of the House of Lords.

Since 1998, there has been a Scottish Parliament in Edinburgh, which is a national, unicameral legislature for Scotland. However, the Scottish Parliament does not have complete power over Scottish Politics, as it only holds the powers which were devolved to it by Westminster in 1997. It cannot legislate on defence issues, currency, or national taxation (e.g. VAT, or Income Tax). Additionally, the Scottish Parliament can be dissolved at any given time by the British Parliament without the consent of the devolved government. This applies to all devolved governments within the United Kingdom, a limit on the sovereignty of the devolved governments.

List of national parliaments

Parliaments of the European Union

The centre block of the Parliament of Canada Building in Ottawa.

The Reichstag building in Berlin.

Bernini's Palazzo Montecitorio in Rome, seat of Italian Parliament.

- European Parliament
- Parliament of Austria (consisting of the National Council and the Federal Council)
- Federal Parliament of Belgium (consisting of the Chamber of Representatives and the Senate)
- Parliament of Bulgaria
- Parliament of Cyprus
- Parliament of the Czech Republic
- Parliament of Denmark
- Parliament of Estonia [*Riigikogu*]
- Parliament of Finland
- Parliament of France (consisting of the National Assembly and the Senate)
- Federal Parliament of Germany (consisting of the Federal Diet and the Federal Council)
- Parliament of Greece
- Parliament of Hungary (*Országház or Parlament*)
- Parliament of Ireland [*Oireachtas*] (consisting of the President of Ireland, the House of Representatives and the Senate)
- Parliament of Italy (consisting of the Chamber of Deputies and the Senate)
- Parliament of Latvia
- Parliament of Lithuania
- Parliament of Luxembourg
- Parliament of Malta
- Parliament of the Netherlands (consisting of the House of Representatives and the Senate)
- Parliament of Poland (consisting of the Sejm and the Senate)
- Parliament of Portugal
- Parliament of Romania (consisting of the Chamber of Deputies and the Senate)
- Parliament of Slovakia
- Parliament of Slovenia (consisting of the National Assembly and the National Council)

- Parliament of Spain (consisting of the Congress of Deputies and the Senate)
- Parliament of Sweden
- Parliament of the United Kingdom (consisting of the House of Commons and the House of Lords)

The Hungarian Parliament Building in Budapest

Others

- Parliament of Albania
- Parliament of Australia
  - The federal (Commonwealth) government of Australia has a bicameral **parliament**, and each of Australia's six states has a bicameral **parliament** except for Queensland, which has a unicameral parliament.
- Parliament of Bangladesh
- Parliament of Barbados
- Parliament of Canada (consisting of the House of Commons and the Senate)
  - The federal government of Canada has a bicameral **parliament**, and each of Canada's 10 provinces has a unicameral **parliament**.
- National People's Congress of the People's Republic of China
  - Legislative Council of Hong Kong

Austrian Parliament Building in Vienna

- Parliament of Croatia
- Parliament of the Faroe Islands
- Parliament of Fiji
- Parliament of Georgia (საქართველოს პარლამენტი/sakartvelos p'arlament'i, Abkhaz: АҚЫРҬШӘЫЛА АПАРЛАМЕНТ, akyrtshwyla ap'arlament')
- Parliament of Ghana
- Parliament of Iceland (The Icelandic Althing and the Manx Tynwald share the claim of the oldest parliaments in the world.)[23]

Parliament of Bangladesh in Dhaka

- Parliament of India (consisting of the Lok Sabha and the Rajya Sabha)
- Parliament of Indonesia
- Parliament of Iran
- Parliament of Iraq
- Parliament of Japan (Diet) (consisting of the House of Representatives and the House of Councillors)
- Parliament of Lebanon
- Parliament of the Isle of Man – Tynwald (Manx: *Tinvaal*) (The Icelandic Althing and the Manx Tynwald share the claim of the oldest parliaments in the world.)[23]

Neoclassical portico of São Bento Palace, the Parliament of Portugal.

- Parliament of Israel – *Knesset*
- Parliament of Malaysia
- Parliament of Montenegro
- Parliament of Morocco
- Parliament of Nauru

- Parliament of Nepal (recently reorganised)
- Parliament of New Zealand
- Parliament of North Korea (Supreme People's Assembly)
- Parliament of Norway (*Storting*)
- Parliament of Pakistan
- Parliament of the Philippines (Congress)
- Sapmi Parliament
- Parliament of Scotland
- Parliament of Serbia
- Parliament of Singapore
- Parliament of South Africa
- Parliament of South Korea (National Assembly)
- Parliament of Sri Lanka
- Federal Parliament of Switzerland (Federal Assembly)
- Parliament of Thailand (National Assembly)
- Parliament of the Central Tibetan Administration
- Parliament of Trinidad and Tobago
- Parliament of Turkey (Grand National Assembly)
- Parliament of the United States (Congress) (consisting of the House of Representatives and the Senate)
- Parliament of Ukraine
- Parliament of Wales (National Assembly)
- Parliament of Zimbabwe

The National Diet Building in Tokyo

Parliament of India, New Delhi

Parliament House of Islamic Republic of Pakistan.

Verkhovna Rada, The Parliament Building of Ukraine.

List of Subnational parliamentary governments

Canada

See: Legislative Assemblies of Canadian provinces and territories

Australia

See: Parliaments of the Australian states and territories

Belgium

In the federal (bicameral) kingdom of Belgium, there is a curious asymmetrical constellation serving as directly elected legislatures for three "territorial" *regions*—Flanders (Dutch), Brussels (bilingual, certain peculiarities of competence, also the only region not comprising any of the 10 provinces) and Wallonia (French)—and three cultural *communities*—Flemish (Dutch, competent in Flanders and for the Dutch-speaking inhabitants of Brussels), Francophone (French, for Wallonia and for Francophones in Brussels) and German (for speakers of that language in a few designated municipalities in the east of the Walloon Region, living alongside Francophones but under two different regimes)

- Vlaams Parliament ("Flemish Parliament"; originally styled Vlaamse Raad "Flemish Council") served both the Flemish Community (whose same it uses) and, in application of a Belgian constitutional option, of the region of Flanders (in all matters of regional competence, its decisions have no effect in Brussels)
- Parliament of the French Community
- parliament of the German Community
- parliament of the Walloon region
- parliament of the Brussels 'capital' region;

  within the capital's regional assembly however, there also exist two so-called *Community Commissions* (fixed numbers, not an automatic repartition of the regional assembly), a Dutch-speaking one and a Francophone one, for various matters split up by linguistic community but under Brussels' regional competence, and even 'joint community commissions' consisting of both for certain institutions that could be split up but are not.

Assembly of Deputies, The Parliament Building of Lebanon.

Majlis Al-Umma (مجلس الأمة, "The Council of the Nation"), the Kuwaiti parliament, in Kuwait City

Denmark

- Parliament of Greenland
- Løgting

Finland

- Parliament of Åland

Germany

- State legislatures of Germany

The Netherlands

- States-Provincial

Norway

see subnational parliamentary system in Norway

Spain

See: List of Spanish regional legislatures

United Kingdom

- Parliament of the United Kingdom
- Northern Ireland Assembly
- Scottish Parliament
- Welsh Assembly

Other parliaments

Contemporary supranational parliaments

List is not exhaustive

- Pan-African Parliament
- Central American Parliament
- Latin American Parliament
- European Parliament

Equivalent national legislatures

- Majlis, e.g. in Iran
- in Afghanistan: Wolesi Jirga (elected, legislative lower house) and Meshrano Jirga (mainly advisory, indirect representation); in special cases, e.g. as constituent assembly, a Loya Jirga
- in Indonesia: People's Consultative Assembly, consists of People's Representative Council (elected, legislative lower house) and Regional Representative Council (elected, legislative upper house with limited powers)

Defunct

- Parliament of Ireland (1297–1801)
- Parliament of Southern Ireland (1921–1922)
- People's Parliament (1940s)
- Silesian Parliament (1922–1945)
- Parliament of Northern Ireland (1921–1973)
- Batasang Pambansa (1978-1986)
- National Assembly of the Republic of China (1913–2005)

See also

- Congress
- Delegated legislation
- Democratic mundialization
- Government
- History of democracy
- Inter-Parliamentary Union
- Legislation
- Parliamentary procedure
- Parliamentary records
- Magnum Concilium
- Witan
- Parliament of the World's Religions
- List of current presidents of assembly

References

[1] Political System (http://www.britannica.com/EBchecked/topic/467746/political-system) Encyclopædia Britannica Online
[2] Jacobsen, T. (July 1943). "Primitive Democracy in Ancient Mesopotamia". Journal of Near Eastern Studies 2 (3): 159–172.
[3] Robinson, E. W. (1997) The First Democracies: Early Popular Government Outside Athens (http://books.google.com/books?id=T1kfcobFRSMC) Franz Steiner Verlag. ISBN 3-515-06951-8.
[4] Bailkey, N. (July 1967). "Early Mesopotamian Constitutional Development". American History Review 72 (4): 1211–1236. http://www.jstor.org/pss/1847791.
[5] Larsen, J.A.O. (Jan. 1973). "Demokratia". Classical Philology 68 (1): 45–46.
[6] de Sainte, C.G.E.M. (2006). The Class Struggle in the Ancient Greek World. Cornell University Press. ISBN 0-8014-1442-3. http://books.google.com/books?id=LkYIAAAAIAAJ.
[7] Bongard-Levin, G.M. (1986). A complex study of Ancient India. South Asia Books. ISBN 81-202-0141-8.
[8] Sharma, J.P. (1968). Aspects of Political Ideas and Institutions in Ancient India. Motilal Banarsidass Publ.. http://books.google.com/books?id=sQKNAAAAMAAJ.
[9] John Dunn:*Democracy:a History*,p.24 (http://books.google.es/books?id=ccoOfhyjFNEC&printsec=frontcover&dq=democracy+a+history&cd=1#v=onepage&q=athens&f=false)
[10] Abbott, Frank Frost (1901). A History and Description of Roman Political Institutions. Elibron Classics. ISBN 0-543-92749-0.
[11] Byrd, Robert (1995). The Senate of the Roman Republic. US Government Printing Office Senate Document 103–23.
[12] "The Shura principle in Islam" by Sadek Jawad Sulaiman (http://www.alhewar.com/SadekShura.htm)
[13] *The System of Islam, (Nidham ul Islam)* by Taqiuddin an-Nabhani (http://www.hizb-ut-tahrir.org/PDF/EN/en_books_pdf/system_of_islam.pdf), Al-Khilafa Publications, 1423 AH – 2002 CE, p.61
[14] *The System of Islam*, by Taqiuddin an-Nabhani (http://www.hizb-ut-tahrir.org/PDF/EN/en_books_pdf/system_of_islam.pdf), p.39
[15] *Shura and Democracy*,by M. A. Muqtedar Khan (http://www.ijtihad.org/shura.htm)
[16] Liebermann, Felix, The National Assembly in the Anglo-Saxon Period (Halle, 1913; repr. New York, 1961).
[17] Birth of the english Parliament (http://www.parliament.uk/about/living-heritage/evolutionofparliament/originsofparliament/birthofparliament/overview/origins/)
[19] Michael Burger: The Shaping of Western Civilization: From Antiquity To the Enlightenment. Page: 190
[20] Susana Galera: Judicial Review: A Comparative Analysis Inside the European Legal System. Page: 21
[21] Gaines Post: Studies in Medieval Legal Thought: Public Law And the State, 1100-1322 Page 62
[23] . The webpage contains a partial transcription of the following book:

External links

- The International Association of Business and Parliament (IABP) Scottish Scheme (http://www.iabp.org/)
- United Kingdom Parliament (http://www.webcitation.org/5hP7hkahY)

Book_of_Common_Prayer

The **Book of Common Prayer** is the short title of a number of related prayer books used in the Anglican Communion, as well as by the Continuing Anglican, "Anglican realignment" and other Anglican churches. The original book, published in 1549 , in the reign of Edward VI, was a product of the English Reformation following the break with Rome. Prayer books, unlike books of prayers, contain the words of structured (or liturgical) services of worship. The work of 1549 was the first prayer book to include the complete forms of service for daily and Sunday worship in English. It contained Morning Prayer, Evening Prayer, the Litany, and Holy Communion and also the occasional services in full: the orders for Baptism, Confirmation, Marriage, 'prayers to be said with the sick' and a Funeral service. It also set out in full the "propers" (that is the parts of the service which varied week by week or, at times, daily throughout the Church's Year): the collects and the epistle and gospel readings for the Sunday Communion Service. Old Testament and New Testament readings for daily prayer were specified in tabular format as were the Psalms; and canticles, mostly biblical, that were provided to be said or sung between the readings .

The 1549 book was soon succeeded by a more reformed revision in 1552 under the same editorial hand, that of Thomas Cranmer, Archbishop of Canterbury. It was used only for a few months, as after Edward VI's death in 1553, his half-sister Mary I restored Roman Catholic worship. She herself died in 1558, and in 1559 Elizabeth I reintroduced the 1552 book with a few modifications to make it acceptable to more traditionally minded worshippers, notably the inclusion of the words of administration from the 1549 Communion Service alongside those of 1552.

In 1604 James I ordered some further changes, the most significant of these being the addition to the Catechism of a section on the Sacraments. Following the tumultuous events leading to and including the English Civil War, another major revision was published in 1662 . That edition has remained the official prayer book of the Church of England, although in the 21st century, an alternative book called *Common Worship* has largely displaced the *Book of Common Prayer* at the main Sunday worship service of most English parish churches.

A *Book of Common Prayer* with local variations is used in churches inside and outside the Anglican Communion in over 50 different countries and in over 150 different languages . In many parts of the world, other books have replaced it in regular weekly worship.

Traditional English Lutheran, Methodist and Presbyterian prayer books have borrowed from the *Book of Common Prayer*, and the marriage and burial rites have found their way into those of other denominations and into the English language. Like the Authorized King James Bible and the works of Shakespeare, many words and phrases from the *Book of Common Prayer* have entered common parlance.

Full name

The full name of the 1662 **Book of Common Prayer** is *The Book of Common Prayer and Administration of the Sacraments and other Rites and Ceremonies of the Church according to the use of the Church of England together with the Psalter or Psalms of David pointed as they are to be sung or said in churches and the form and manner of making, ordaining, and consecrating of bishops, priests, and deacons.*

History

Background

The forms of parish worship in the late medieval church in England, which followed the Latin Roman Rite, varied according to local practice. By far the most common form, or "use", found in Southern England was that of Sarum (Salisbury). There was no single book; the services that would be provided by the Book of Common Prayer were to be found in the Missal (the Eucharist), the Breviary (daily offices), Manual (the occasional services of Baptism,

Marriage, Burial etc.), and Pontifical (services appropriate to a bishop—Confirmation, Ordination). The chant (plainsong, plainchant) for worship was contained in the Roman Gradual for the Mass and in the Antiphoner for the offices. The Book of Common Prayer has never contained prescribed music or chant, however John Merbecke produced his *Book of Common Praier noted* in 1550 which set what would have been the proper of the Mass (Kyrie, Gloria, Creed, etc.) in the new BCP to simple plainchant inspired by Sarum Use. The work of producing a liturgy in the English language books was largely done by Thomas Cranmer, Archbishop of Canterbury, starting cautiously in the reign of Henry VIII, and then more radically under his son Edward VI. In his early days Cranmer was somewhat conservative, an admirer, if a critical one, of John Fisher. It may have been his visit to Germany in 1532 (where he secretly married) which began the change in his outlook. Then in 1538, as Henry began diplomatic negotiations with Lutheran princes, Cranmer came face to face with a Lutheran embassy . The Exhortation and Litany, the earliest English-language service of the Church of England, was the first overt manifestation of his changing views. It was no mere translation from the Latin: its Protestant character is made clear by the drastic reduction of the place of saints, compressing what had been the major part into three petitions . Published in 1544, it borrowed greatly from Martin Luther's Litany and Myles Coverdale's New Testament and was the only service that might be considered to be "Protestant" to be finished within the lifetime of King Henry VIII.

Prayer Books of Edward VI

1549

Cranmer's 1549 Book of Common Prayer

It was not until Henry's death in 1547 and the accession of Edward VI that revision could proceed faster. Cranmer finished his work on an English Communion rite in 1548, obeying an order of Convocation of the previous year that communion was to be given to the people as both bread and wine. The ordinary Roman Rite of the Mass had made no provision for any congregation present to receive communion. So, Cranmer composed in English an additional rite of congregational preparation and communion (based on the form of the Sarum rite for Communion of the Sick), to be undertaken immediately following the communion, in both kinds, of the priest.

Further developed, and fully translated into English, this Communion service was included, one year later, in 1549, in a full prayer book, set out with daily offices, readings for Sundays and Holy Days, the Communion Service, Public Baptism, of Confirmation, of Matrimony, The Visitation of the Sick, At a Burial and the Ordinal (added in 1550) . The Preface to this edition, which contained Cranmer's explanation as to why a new prayer book was necessary, began: "There was never any thing by the wit of man so well devised, or so sure established, which in continuance of time hath not been corrupted." Although the work is commonly attributed to Cranmer, its detailed origins are obscure . A group of bishops and divines met first at Chertsey and then at Windsor in 1548, drawn from both conservatives and reformers, agreed only "the service of the church ought to be in the mother tongue" . Cranmer collected the material from many sources; even the opening of Preface (above) was borrowed . He borrowed much from German sources, particularly from work commissioned by Hermann von Wied, Archbishop of Cologne; and also from Osiander (to whom he was related by marriage) . The Church Order of Brandenberg and Nuremberg was partly the work of the latter. Many phrases are characteristic of the German reformer Martin Bucer, or of the Italian

Peter Martyr, (who was staying with Cranmer at the time of the finalising of drafts), or of his chaplain, Thomas Becon. However, to Cranmer is "credited the overall job of editorship and the overarching structure of the book" including the systematic amendment of his materials to remove any idea that human merit contributed to their salvation .

The Communion service of 1549 maintained the format of distinct rites of consecration and communion, that had been introduced the previous year; but with the Latin rite of the Mass (chiefly following the familiar structure in the Use of Sarum), translated into English. By outwardly maintaining familiar forms, Cranmer hoped to establish the practice of weekly congregational communion, and included exhortations to encourage this; and instructions that communion should never be received by the priest alone. This represented a radical change from late medieval practice—whereby the primary focus of congregational worship was taken to be attendance at the consecration, and adoration of the elevated consecrated host. In late medieval England, congregations regularly received communion only at Easter; and otherwise individual lay people might expect to receive communion only when gravely ill, or in the form of a Nuptial Mass on being married.

Cranmer's work of simplification and revision was also applied to the Daily Offices, which were to become Morning, and Evening Prayer; and which he hoped would also serve as a daily form of prayer to be used by the Laity, thus replacing both the late medieval lay observation of the Latin Hours of the Virgin, and its English equivalent, the *Primer*. This simplification was anticipated by the work of Cardinal Francis Quiñones, a Spanish Franciscan, in his abortive revision of the Roman Breviary published in 1537 . Cranmer took up Quiñones's principle that everything should be sacrificed to secure continuity in singing the Psalter and reading the Bible. His first draft, produced during Henry's reign, retained the traditional seven distinct Canonical hours of Office prayer; but in his second draft, while he retained the Latin, he consolidated these into two . The 1549 book then dispensed with the Latin, and with all non-biblical readings; and established a rigorously biblical cycle of readings for Morning and Evening Prayer (set according to the calendar year, rather than the ecclesiastical year) and a Psalter to be read consecutively throughout each month. He provided that the New Testament (other than the Book of Revelation) be read through three times in a year, while the Old Testament, including the Apocrypha would be read through once. Of the set canticles, only the Te Deum was retained of the non-biblical material.

Introduced on Whitsunday 1549, after considerable debate and revision in Parliament—but there is no evidence that it was ever submitted to either Convocation—it was said to have pleased neither reformers nor their opponents, indeed the Catholic Bishop Gardiner could say of it was that it "was patient of a catholic interpretation". It was clearly unpopular in the parishes of Devon and Cornwall where, along with severe social problems, its introduction was one of the causes of the "commotions", or rebellions in the summer of that year, partly because many Cornish people lacked sufficient English to understand it ,. [It appears that it was far less significant in the other "commotions" in the Home Counties and the "Eastern Rebellion".] Particularly unpopular was the banning of processions and the sending out of commissioners to enforce the new requirements. There was widespread opposition to the introduction of regular congregational Communion, partly because the extra costs of bread and wine that would fall on the parish; but mainly out of an intense resistance to undertaking in regular worship, a religious practice previously associated with marriage or illness.

1552

Cranmer's Prayer book of 1552

The 1549 book was, from the outset, intended only as a temporary expedient, as Bucer was assured having met Cranmer for the first time in April 1549: 'concessions...made both as a respect for antiquity and to the infirmity of the present age' as he wrote . Both Bucer and Peter Martyr wrote detailed proposals for modification; Bucer's *Censura* ran to 28 chapters which influenced Cranmer significantly though he did not follow them slavishly and the new book was duly produced in 1552, making "fully perfect" what was already implicit . The policy of incremental reform was now unveiled: more Roman Catholic practices were now excised, as doctrines had in 1549 been subtly changed. Thus, in the Eucharist, gone were the words Mass and altar; the 'Lord have mercy' was interleaved into a recitation of the Ten Commandments and the Gloria was removed to the end of the service. The Eucharistic prayer was split in two so that Eucharistic bread and wine were shared immediately after the words of institution (This is my Body..This is my blood...in remembrance of me.); while its final element, the Prayer of Oblation, (with its reference to an offering of a 'Sacrifice of praise and thanksgiving'), was transferred, much changed, to a position after the priest and congregation had received Communion, and was made optional with an alternative prayer of thanksgiving provided. The Elevation of the Host had been forbidden in 1549; all manual acts were now omitted. The words at the administration of Communion which, in the prayer book of 1549 described the Eucharistic species as 'The body of our Lorde Jesus Christe...', 'The blood of our Lorde Jesus Christe...' were replaced with the words 'Take, eat, in remembrance that Christ died for thee..' etc. The Peace, at which in the early Church the congregation had exchanged a greeting, was removed altogether. Vestments such as the stole, chasuble and cope were no longer to be worn, but only a surplice. It was the final stage of the reformers' work of removing all elements of sacrificial offering from the Latin Mass; so that it should cease to be seen as a ritual at which the priest, on behalf of the faithful offered Christ's body and blood to God; and might rather be seen as a ritual whereby Christ shared his body and blood, according to a different sacramental theology, with the faithful.

Cranmer recognized that the 1549 rite of Communion had been capable of conservative misinterpretation and misuse in that the consecration rite might still be undertaken even when no congregational Communion followed. Consequently, in 1552 he thoroughly integrated Consecration and Communion into a single rite, with congregational preparation preceding the words of institution—such that it would not be possible to mimic the Mass with the priest communicating alone. He appears nevertheless, to have been resigned to being unable for the present to establish in parishes the weekly practice of receiving Communion; so he restructured the service so as to allow ante-Communion as a distinct rite of worship—following the Communion rite through the readings and offertory, as far as the intercessory "Prayer for the Church Militant".

Diarmaid MacCulloch suggests that Cranmer's own Eucharistic theology in these years approximated most closely to that of Heinrich Bullinger; but that he intended the Prayer Book to be acceptable to the widest range of Reformed Eucharistic belief, including the high sacramental theology of Bucer and John Calvin . At the same time, however, Cranmer intended that constituent parts of the rites gathered into the Prayer Book should still, so far as possible, be recognizably derived from traditional forms and elements.

In the Baptism service the signing with the cross was moved until after the baptism and the exorcism, the anointing, the putting on of the chrysom robe and the triple immersion were omitted. Most drastic of all was the removal of the Burial service from church: it was to take place at the graveside. In 1549, there had been provision for a Requiem (not so called) and prayers of commendation and committal, the first addressed to the deceased. All that remained was a single reference to the deceased, giving thanks for their delivery from 'the myseryes of this sinneful world'. This new Order for the Burial of the Dead was a drastically stripped-down memorial service designed to undermine definitively the whole complex of traditional beliefs about Purgatory and intercessory prayer .

In other respects, however, both the Baptism and Burial services imply a theology of salvation that accords notably less with Reformed teachings than do the counterpart passages in the Articles of Religion. In the Burial service, the possibility that a deceased person who has died in the faith may nevertheless not be counted amongst God's elect, is not entertained. In the Baptism service the priest explicitly pronounces the baptised infant as being now *regenerate*. In both cases, conformity with strict Reformed Protestant principles would have resulted in a conditional formulation. The continued inconsistency between the Articles of Religion and the Prayer Book remained a point of contention for Puritans; and would in the 19th century come close to tearing the Church of England apart, through the course of the Gorham judgement.

The Orders of Morning and Evening Prayer were extended by the inclusion of a penitential section at the beginning including a corporate confession of sin and a general absolution, although the text was printed only in Morning Prayer with rubrical directions to use it in the evening as well. The general pattern of Bible reading in 1549 was retained (as it was in 1559) except that distinct Old and New Testament readings were now specified for Morning and Evening Prayer on certain feast days. Following the publication of the 1552 Prayer Book, a revised English Primer was published in 1553; adapting the Offices and Morning and Evening Prayer, and other prayers, for lay domestic piety .

English Prayer Book in the reign of Mary I

The 1552 book, however, was used only for a short period, as Edward VI had died in the summer of 1553 and, as soon as she could do so, Mary I, restored union with Rome. The Latin Mass was re-established, altars, roods and statues were reinstated; an attempt was made to restore the English Church to its Roman affiliation. Cranmer was punished for his work in the English Reformation by being burned at the stake on 21 March 1556. Nevertheless, the 1552 book was to survive. After Mary's death in 1558, it became the primary source for the Elizabethan Book of Common Prayer, with subtle if significant changes only.

Hundreds of Protestants fled into exile—establishing an English church in Frankfurt am Main. A bitter and very public dispute ensued between those, such as Edmund Grindal and Richard Cox, who wished to preserve in exile the exact form of worship of the 1552 Prayer Book; and those, such as John Knox the minister of the congregation, who regarded that book as still partially tainted with compromise. Eventually, in 1555, the civil authorities expelled Knox and his supporters to Geneva, where they adopted a new prayer book, *The Form of Prayers*, which derived principally from Calvin's French *La Forme des Prières* . Consequently, when the accession of Elizabeth I re-asserted the dominance of the reformed Church of England, there remained a significant body of more Protestant believers who were nevertheless hostile to the Book of Common Prayer. John Knox took *The Form of Prayers* with him to Scotland, where it formed the basis of the Scottish *Book of Common Order*.

1559 Prayer Book

Thus, under Elizabeth, a more permanent enforcement of the reformed Church of England was undertaken and the 1552 book was republished in 1559, scarcely altered .

Prayer book of 1559.

The alterations, though minor, were however to cast a long shadow. One, the "Ornaments Rubric", related to what was worn. Instead of the banning of all vestments except the rochet for bishops and the surplice for parish clergy, it permitted "such ornaments...as were in use...in the second year of K. Edward VI". This allowed substantial leeway for more traditionalist clergy to retain some of the vestments which they felt were appropriate to liturgical celebration (at least until the Queen gave further instructions under the Act of Uniformity of 1559). It was to be the basis of claims in the 19th century that vestments such as chasubles, albs and stoles were legal. At Holy Communion, the words from the 1549 book, "the Body of our Lord Jesus Christ" etc. were combined with the words of Edward's second book, "Take eat in remembrance" etc. The instruction to the congregation to kneel when receiving communion was retained; but the accompanying Black Rubric denying any "real and essential presence" of Christ's flesh and blood, was removed . The conservative nature of these changes underlines the fact that reformed principles were by no means universally popular – a fact that the Queen herself recognised: her revived Act of Supremacy, giving her the ambiguous title of Supreme Governor, passed without difficulty but the Act of Uniformity 1559, giving statutory force to the Prayer Book, passed through the House of Lords by only three votes. It made constitutional history in being imposed by the laity alone, as all the bishops, except those imprisoned by the Queen and unable to attend, voted against it . Convocation had made its position clear by affirming the traditional doctrine of the Eucharist, the authority of the Pope, and the reservation by divine law to clergy "of handling and defining concerning the things belonging to faith, sacraments, and discipline ecclesiastical" .

After the several innovations and reversals, the new forms of worship took time to settle in. Among Cranmer's innovations, retained in the new book was the requirement of weekly Holy Communion services. In practice, as before the English Reformation, many received communion rarely, as little as once a year in some cases; George Herbert estimated it as no more than six times. . Practice, however, varied from place to place: very high attendance at festivals was the order of the day in many parishes and in some regular communion was very popular, in other places families stayed away or sent "a servant to be the liturgical representative of their household." . Few parish clergy were initially licensed to preach by the bishops; in the absence of a licensed preacher, Sunday services were required to be accompanied by reading one of the homilies written by Cranmer . George Herbert was, however, not alone in his enthusiasm for preaching, which he regarded as one of the prime functions of a parish priest . Music was much simplified and a radical distinction developed between, on the one hand, parish worship where only the metrical psalms of Sternhold and Hopkins might be sung and, on the other hand, worship in churches with organs and surviving choral foundations, where the music of John Marbeck and others was developed into a rich choral tradition . The whole act of parish worship might take well over two hours; and accordingly, churches were equipped with pews in which households could sit together (whereas in the medieval church, men and women had worshipped separately). Diarmaid MacCulloch describes the new act of worship as, "a morning marathon of prayer, scripture reading, and praise, consisting of mattins, litany, and ante-communion, preferably as the matrix for a sermon to proclaim the message of scripture anew week by week." .

Many ordinary churchgoers—that is those who could afford a copy as it was expensive—would own a copy of the prayer book. Judith Maltby cites a story of parishioners at Flixton in Suffolk who brought their own prayer books to church in order to shame their vicar into conforming with it: they eventually ousted him . Between 1549 and 1642, roughly 290 editions of the prayer book were produced . Before the end of the Civil War and the introduction of the 1662 prayer book, something like a half a million prayer books are estimated to have been in circulation .

A (re)translation into Latin of the 1559 Book of Common Prayer was made in the form of Walter Haddon's *Liber Precum Publicarum* of 1560. Its use was destined for the universities.

Changes in 1604

On Elizabeth's death in 1603, the 1559 book, substantially that of 1552 which had been regarded as offensive by some, such as Bishop Stephen Gardiner, as being a break with the tradition of the Western Church, had come to be regarded in some quarters as unduly Catholic. On his accession and following the so-called "Millenary Petition", James I called the Hampton Court Conference in 1604—the same meeting of bishops and Puritan divines that initiated the Authorized version of the Bible. This was in effect a series of two conferences: (i) between James and the bishops; (ii) between James and the Puritans on the following day. The Puritans raised four areas of concern: purity of doctrine; the means of maintaining it; church government; and the Book of Common Prayer. Here Confirmation, the cross in baptism, private baptism, the use of the surplice, kneeling for communion, reading the *Apocrypha*; and subscription to the BCP and Articles were all touched on. On the third day, after James had received a report back from the bishops and made final modifications, he announced his decisions to the Puritans and bishops.

The business of making the changes was then entrusted to a small committee of bishops and the Privy Council and, apart from tidying up details, this committee introduced into Morning and Evening Prayer a prayer for the Royal Family; added several thanksgivings to the Occasional Prayers at the end of the Litany; altered the rubrics of Private Baptism limiting it to the minister of the parish, or some other lawful minister, but still allowing it in private houses (the Puritans had wanted it only in the church); and added to the Catechism the section on the sacraments. The changes were put into effect by means of an explanation issued by James in the exercise of his prerogative under the terms of the 1559 Act of Uniformity and Act of Supremacy.

The accession of Charles I (1625–1649) brought about a complete change in the religious scene in that the new king used his supremacy over the established church "to promote his own idiosyncratic style of sacramental Kingship" which was "a very weird aberration from the first hundred years of the early reformed Church of England". He questioned "the populist and parliamentary basis of the Reformation Church" and unsettled to a great extent "the consensual accommodation of Anglicanism" and this led to the Civil War and republican Commonwealth.

With the defeat of Charles I (1625–1649) in the Civil War, the Puritan pressure, exercised through a much-changed Parliament, had increased. Puritan-inspired petitions for the removal of the prayer book and episcopacy "root and branch" resulted in local disquiet in many places and, eventually, the production of locally organized counter petitions. The parliamentary government had its way but it became clear that the division was not between Catholics and Protestants, but between Puritans and those who valued the Elizabethan settlement. . The 1604 book was finally outlawed by Parliament in 1645 to be replaced by the Directory of Public Worship, which was more a set of instructions than a prayer book. How widely the Directory was used is not certain; there is some evidence of its having been purchased, in churchwardens' accounts, but not widely. The Prayer Book certainly was used clandestinely in some places, not least because the Directory made no provision at all for burial services. Following the execution of Charles I in 1649 and the establishment of the Commonwealth under Lord Protector Cromwell, it would not be reinstated until shortly after the restoration of the monarchy to England.

John Evelyn records, in *Diary*, receiving communion according to the 1604 Prayer Book rite:

> *Christmas Day 1657. I went to London with my wife to celebrate Christmas Day... Sermon ended, as [the minister] was giving us the holy sacrament, the chapel was surrounded with soldiers, and all the*

communicants and assembly surprised and kept prisoners by them, some in the house, others carried away... These wretched miscreants held their muskets against us as we came up to receive the sacred elements, as if they would have shot us at the altar.

Changes made in Scotland

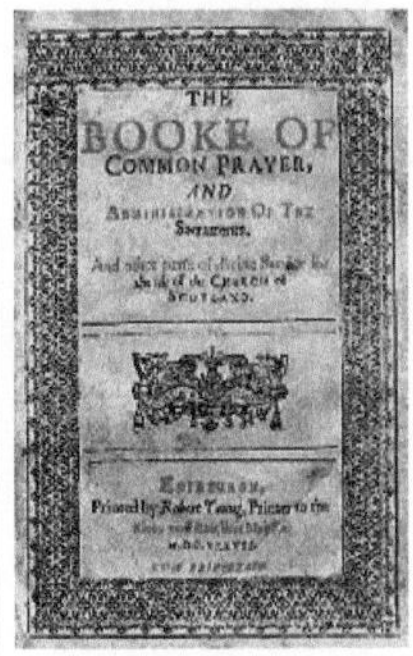

Laud's abortive 1637 Prayer book.

In 1557, the Scots Protestant lords had adopted the English Prayer Book of 1552, for reformed worship in Scotland. However, when John Knox returned to Scotland in 1559, he continued to use the *Form of Prayer* he had created for the English exiles in Geneva and, in 1564, this supplanted the *Book of Common Prayer* under the title of the *Book of Common Order.*

Following the accession of King James VI of Scotland to the throne of England his son, King Charles I, with the assistance of Archbishop Laud, sought to impose the prayer book on Scotland . The book concerned was not, however, the 1559 book but very much that of 1549, the first book of Edward VI. First used in 1637, it was never accepted, having been violently rejected by the Scots. Following the Wars of the Three Kingdoms (including the English Civil War), the Church of Scotland was re-established on a presbyterian basis but by the Act of Comprehension 1690, the rump of Episcopalians were allowed to hold onto their benefices. For liturgy they looked to Laud's book and in 1724 the first of the "wee bookies" was published, containing, for the sake of economy, the central part of the Communion liturgy beginning with the offertory .

Between then and 1764, when a more formal revised version was published, a number of things happened which were to separate the Scottish Episcopal liturgy more firmly from either the English books of 1549 or 1559. First, informal changes were made to the order of the various parts of the service and inserting words indicating a sacrificial intent to the Eucharist; secondly, as a result of Bishop Rattray's researches into the liturgies of St James and St Clement, published in 1744, the form of the invocation was changed. These changes were incorporated into the 1764 book which was to be the liturgy of the Scottish Episcopal Church (until 1911 when it was revised) but it was to influence the liturgy of the Episcopal Church in the United States. A completely new revision was finished in 1929 and several alternative orders of the Communion service and other services have been prepared since then.

1662

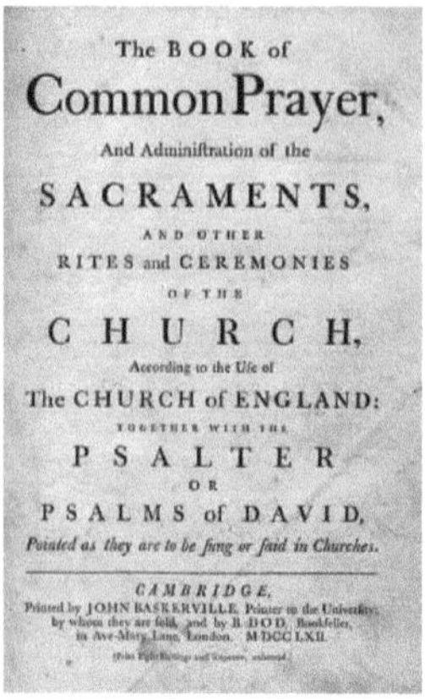
The BOOK of
Common Prayer,
And Administration of the
SACRAMENTS,
AND OTHER
RITES and CEREMONIES
OF THE
CHURCH,
According to the Use of
The CHURCH of ENGLAND:
TOGETHER WITH THE
PSALTER
OR
PSALMS of DAVID,
Pointed as they are to be sung or said in Churches.
CAMBRIDGE,
Printed by JOHN BASKERVILLE, Printer to the University; by whom they are sold, and by B. DOD, Bookseller, in Ave-Mary Lane, London. MDCCLXII.

Title page of the 1662 Prayer Book, printed by John Baskerville in 1762

The 1662 Prayer Book was printed only two years after the restoration of the monarchy, following the Savoy Conference between representative Presbyterians and twelve bishops which was convened by Royal Warrant to "advise upon and review the Book of Common Prayer". Attempts by the Presbyterians, led by Richard Baxter, to gain approval for an alternative service book failed. Their major objections (exceptions) were: firstly, that it was improper for lay people to take any vocal part in prayer (as in the Litany or Lord's Prayer), other than to say "amen"; secondly, that no set prayer should exclude the option of an extempore alternative from the minister; thirdly, that the minister should have the option to omit part of the set liturgy at his discretion; fourthly, that short collects should be replaced by longer prayers and exhortations; and fifthly, that all surviving "Catholic" ceremonial should be removed.

The Savoy Conference ended in disagreement late in July 1661, but the initiative in prayer book revision had already passed to the Convocations and from there to Parliament. The Convocations made some 600 changes, mostly of details, which were "far from partisan or extreme". However, Edwards states that more of the changes suggested by high Anglicans were implemented (though by no means all) and Spurr comments that (except in the case of the Ordinal) the suggestions of the "Laudians" (Cosin and Matthew Wren) were not taken up possibly due to the influence of moderates such as Sanderson and Reynolds. For example, the inclusion in the intercessions of the Communion rite of prayer for the dead was proposed and rejected. The introduction of "Let us pray for the whole state of Christ's Church militant here in earth" remained unaltered and only a thanksgiving for those "departed this life in thy faith and fear" was inserted to introduce the petition that the congregation might be "given grace so to follow their good examples that with them we may be partakers of thy heavenly kingdom". Griffith Thomas commented that the retention of the words "militant here in earth" defines the scope of this petition: we pray for ourselves, we thank God for them, and adduces collateral evidence to this end. Secondly, an attempt was made to restore the Offertory. This was achieved by the insertion of the words "and oblations" into the prayer for the Church and the revision of the rubric so as to require the monetary offerings to be brought to the table (instead of being put in the poor box) and the bread and wine placed upon the table. Previously it had not been clear when and how bread and wine got onto the altar. The so-called "manual acts", whereby the priest took the bread and the cup during the prayer of consecration, which had been deleted in 1552, were restored; and an "amen" was inserted after the words of institution and before communion, hence separating the connections between of consecration and communion which Cranmer had tried to make. After communion, the unused but consecrated bread and wine were to be reverently consumed in church rather than being taken away for the priest's own use. By such subtle means were Cranmer's purposes further confused, leaving it for generations to argue over the precise theology of the rite. One change made that constituted a concession to the Presbyterian Exceptions, was the updating and re-insertion of the so-called "Black Rubric", which had been removed in 1559. This now declared that kneeling in order to receive communion did not imply adoration of the species of the Eucharist nor "to any Corporal Presence of Christ's natural Flesh and Blood"—which, according to the rubric, were in heaven, not here.

Unable to accept the new book, 936 ministers were deprived. (: see [1]) In effect, the 1662 Prayer Book marked the end of a period of just over 100 years, when a common form of liturgy served for almost all reformed public worship in England and the start of the continuing division between Anglicans and Nonconformists. The actual language of the 1662 revision was little changed from that of Cranmer. With two exceptions, some words and phrases which had become archaic were modernised; secondly, the readings for the epistle and gospel at Holy Communion, which had been set out in full since 1549, were now set to the text of the 1611 Authorized Version of the Bible. The Psalter, which had not been printed in the 1549, 1552 or 1559 books—was in 1662 provided in Miles Coverdale's translation from the Great Bible of 1538.

It was this edition which was to be the official *Book of Common Prayer* during the growth of the British Empire and, as a result, has been a great influence on the prayer books of Anglican churches worldwide, liturgies of other denominations in English and of the English language as a whole.

Further attempts at revision

1662–1832

After the 1662 prayer book, development ceased in England until the twentieth century; that it did was, however, a bit of a close run thing. On the death of Charles II his brother, a Roman Catholic, became James II. James wished to achieve toleration for those of his own Roman Catholic faith, whose practices were still banned. This, however, drew the Presbyterians closer to the Church of England in their common desire to resist 'popery'; talk of reconciliation and liturgical compromise was thus in the air. But with the flight of James in 1688 and the arrival of the Calvinist William of Orange the position of the parties changed. The Presbyterians could achieve toleration of their practices without such a right being given to Roman Catholics and without, therefore, their having to submit to the Church of England, even with a liturgy more acceptable to them. They were now in a much stronger position to demand changes that were ever more radical. John Tillotson, Dean of Canterbury pressed the king to set up a Commission to produce such a revision . The so-called *Liturgy of Comprehension* of 1689, which was the result, conceded two thirds of the Presbyterian demands of 1661; but when it came to Convocation the members, now more fearful of William's perceived agenda, did not even discuss it and its contents were, for a long time, not even accessible . This work, however, did go on to influence the prayer books of many British colonies.

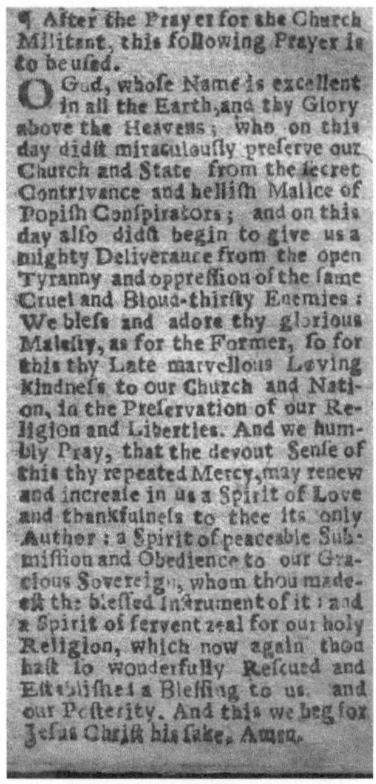

¶ After the Prayer for the Church Militant, this following Prayer is to be uſed.

O God, whoſe Name is excellent in all the Earth, and thy Glory above the Heavens; who on this day didſt miraculouſly preſerve our Church and State from the ſecret Contrivance and helliſh Malice of Popiſh Conſpirators; and on this day alſo didſt begin to give us a mighty Deliverance from the open Tyranny and oppreſſion of the ſame Cruel and Bloud-thirſty Enemies: We bleſs and adore thy glorious Majeſty, as for the Former, ſo for this thy Late marvellous Loving Kindneſs to our Church and Nation, in the Preſervation of our Religion and Liberties. And we humbly Pray, that the devout Senſe of this thy repeated Mercy, may renew and increaſe in us a Spirit of Love and thankfulneſs to thee its only Author: a Spirit of peaceable Submiſſion and Obedience to our Gracious Sovereign, whom thou madeſt the bleſſed Inſtrument of it: and a Spirit of fervent zeal for our holy Religion, which now again thou haſt ſo wonderfully Reſcued and Eſtabliſhed a Bleſſing to us, and our Poſterity. And this we beg for Jeſus Chriſt his ſake, Amen.

A Collect for 5th November, in Book of Common Prayer published London 1689, referring to the Gunpowder Plot and the arrival of William III

1833–1906

Edward Bouverie Pusey, a leader of the Oxford Movement

By the 19th century other pressures upon the book of 1662 had arisen. Adherents of the Oxford Movement, begun in 1833, raised questions about the relationship of the Church of England to the apostolic church and thus about its forms of worship. Known as Tractarians after their production of *Tracts for the Times* on theological issues, they advanced the case for the Church of England being essentially a part of the 'Western Church', of which the Roman Catholic Church was the chief representative. The illegal use of elements of the Roman rite, the use of candles, vestments and incense, practices known as Ritualism, had become widespread and led to the Public Worship Regulation Act 1874 which established a new system of discipline, intending to bring the 'Romanisers' into conformity . The Act had no effect on illegal practices: five clergy were imprisoned for contempt of court and after the trial of the much loved Bishop Edward King of Lincoln, it became clear that some revision of the liturgy had to be embarked upon .

One branch of the ritualistic movement argued that both 'Romanisers' (by imitating the Church of Rome) and their Evangelical opponents (by imitating Reformed churches) transgressed the Ornaments Rubric of 1559, 'that such Ornaments of the Church, and of the Ministers thereof, at all Times of their Ministration, shall be retained, and be in use, as were in this Church of England, by the Authority of Parliament, in the Second Year of the Reign of King Edward the Sixth'. These adherents of ritualism, among whom were Percy Dearmer and others, claimed that the Ornaments Rubric prescribed the ritual usages of the Sarum Rite with the exception of a few minor things already abolished by the early reformation. Following a Royal Commission report in 1906, work began on a new prayer book, work that was to take twenty years due in part to the demands of the Great War (1914–18) and in part to the constitution of the Church Assembly in 1920 which "perhaps not unnaturally wished to do the work all over again for itself."

1906–2000

In 1927, this proposed prayer book reached its final form. So as to reduce conflict with traditionalists to a minimum, it was decided that the form of service to be used would be determined by each congregation. With these open guidelines the book was granted approval by the Church of England Convocations and Church Assembly in July 1927. Since the Church of England Assembly (Powers) Act 1919 required measures affecting the Book of Common Prayer to be approved by Parliament before receiving royal assent, the measure authorising its use together with an annexed copy in the form of a "Deposited Book", was submitted to Parliament. The House of Lords approved the Book by a large majority, but the corresponding resolution in the House of Commons was defeated by thirty-three votes on 15 December 1927 when the MPs William Joynson-Hicks and Rosslyn Mitchell "reached and inflamed all the latent Protestant prejudices in the House" and argued strongly against it on the grounds that the proposed book was "papistical" and was a restoration of the Roman Mass and implied the doctrine of transubstantiation.

Early in the year 1928 a second measure (known as the Prayer Book Measure 1928) was introduced in the Church Assembly proposing to authorise the use of the "Deposited Book" with certain amendments which were set out in a schedule to the Measure. This Measure again was approved by large majorities in both the Convocations and the Church Assembly; but again failed to pass the House of Commons, being defeated by forty-six votes on 14 June 1928. Writing in 1947, Cyril Garbett comments:

> "The House of Commons was within its constitutional rights in rejecting in a few hours the work of many anxious years. Nonconformist members and members from constituencies which would not have been affected by the Revised Book were only exercising their full legal rights in throwing out a Measure which was approved by the majority of English Members of Parliament. But whatever were the reasons behind the votes of the majority, the rejection of the Measures made it plain that the Church does not possess full spiritual freedom to determine its worship ..."

Stephen Neill points out that the Roman Catholic members of parliament abstained from voting.

In response to this rejection, the bishops issued a unanimous statement, asserting the Church of England's right to order its forms of worship and, in 1929, the Upper House of the Convocation of Canterbury resolved that bishops might approve the use of the 1928 book, notwithstanding the lack of parliamentary authority. It became common for prayer books to be printed with the 1662 and 1928 forms of service in parallel columns, although the legal basis of the revision remained unclear. The 1928 revised forms of Matrimony and Baptism were quite widely adopted, but those of other rites tended not to be; the consequence, in practice, being very wide variation in liturgical practice from parish to parish, with very few clergy adhering consistently to the strict observation of either the 1662 or the 1928 forms of worship.

The effect of the failure of the 1928 book was salutary: no further attempts were made to revise the *Book of Common Prayer*. Instead a different process, that of producing an alternative book, led to the publication of Series 1, 2 and 3 in the 1960s, the 1980 Alternative Service Book and subsequently to the 2000 *Common Worship* series of books. Both differ substantially from the *Book of Common Prayer,* though the latter includes in the Order Two form of the Holy Communion a very slight revision of the prayer book service, largely along the lines proposed for the 1928 Prayer Book. Order One follows the pattern of modern liturgical scholarship.

Since 2001

In 2003, a Roman Catholic liturgical book, the *Book of Divine Worship*, was published in the United States. It is composed of material drawn from the proposed 1928 book, the 1979 *Book of Common Prayer of the Episcopal Church in the United States of America and the Roman Missal. Former Anglicans within the Anglican Use published it primarily for their own use.*

In the Anglican Communion

With British colonial expansion from the 17th century onwards, Anglicanism was planted across the globe. These new Anglican churches at first used and then revised the use of the Book of Common Prayer, until they, like the English church, produced prayer books which took into account the developments in liturgical study and practice in the 19th and 20th centuries which come under the general heading of the Liturgical Movement.

Africa

The Book Of Common Prayer in Africa is the same as the ones in other places. Each province or national church has its own signature which is put on the cover pages of the book as there are some words that differ from one province to another. In Yoruba it is known as *Iwe Adura ti gbogbo Ijo Anglikan*.

Asia

China and Hong Kong

Europe

Ireland

William Bedell had undertaken an Irish translation of the Book of Common Prayer in 1606. An Irish translation of the revised prayer book of 1662 was effected by John Richardson (1664–1747) and published in 1712. It has been revised several times, and the present edition has been used since 2004.

The English-Chinese Diglot Book of Common Prayers, used by the Filipino-Chinese community of St Stephen's Pro-Cathedral

Wales

An Act of Parliament passed in the year 1563, entitled "An Act for the Translating of the Bible and the Divine Service into the Welsh Tongue," ordered that the Old and New Testament, together with the Book of Common Prayer, were to be translated into Welsh. A translation by Richard Davies, bishop of St David's and the scholar William Salesbury was published in 1567 by Humphrey Toy as *Y Llyfr Gweddi Gyffredin*. A new revision — probably by Bishop George Griffith (1601–1666), of St Asaph - based on the revised English book of 1662, was published in 1664.[2]

Even after the creation of the Church in Wales 1920, the 1662 book (and its Welsh equivalent) was used until 1966, when trials of new services began. The current book was published in 1984, and is currently under revision.

Isle of Man

The first Manx translation of the Book of Common Prayer was made by Bishop John Phillips of Sodor and Man in 1610. A more successful "New Version" by Bishop Mark Hildesley (1698–1772) was in use until 1824 when English liturgy became universal on the island.[2]

Oceania

Australia

The **Anglican Church of Australia**, until 1981 officially known as the *Church of England in Australia and Tasmania*, became self-governing in 1961. Among other things the General Synod agreed that the Book of Common Prayer was to "be regarded as the authorised standard of worship and doctrine in this Church ...". In 1978 *An Australian Prayer Book* was produced which sought to adhere to this principle, so that where the Liturgical Committee could not agree on a formulation, the words or expressions of the BCP were to be used . The result was conservative revision.

In 1995 a similar process could be observed as elsewhere with the production of *A Prayer Book for Australia* which departed from both the structure and wording of the BCP. The process was accompanied by numerous objections, notably from the deeply conservative evangelical Diocese of Sydney which noted the loss of BCP wording and of an explicit "biblical doctrine of substitutionary atonement". The Diocese of Sydney has developed its own small prayer book, called *Sunday Services*, to supplement the existing prayer book and preserve the original theology which the Sydney diocese asserts has been changed.

North and Central America

Canada

The **Anglican Church of Canada** developed its first Book of Common Prayer separately from the English version in 1918, which received final authorization from General Synod on April 16, 1922.[3] The revision of 1959 was much more substantial, bearing a family relationship to that of the abortive 1928 book in England. The language was conservatively modernized, and additional seasonal material was added. As in England, while many prayers were retained the structure of the Communion service was altered: a Prayer of Oblation was added to the Eucharistic prayer after the 'words of institution', thus reflecting the rejection of Cranmer's theology in liturgical developments across the Anglican Communion. More controversially, the Psalter included in the book omitted certain sections, including the entirety of Psalm 58.[4] General Synod gave final authorization to the revision in 1962, to coincide with the 300th anniversary of the 1662 Book of Common Prayer. A French translation, *Le Recueil des Prières de la Communauté Chrétienne*, was published in 1967.

After a period of experimentation with the publication of various supplements, the *Book of Alternative Services* was published in 1985. This book (which owes much to Roman Catholic, Lutheran, Anglican and other sources) has widely supplanted the 1959 book, though the latter remains authorized. As in other places, there has been a reaction and the Canadian version of the Book of Common Prayer has found supporters.

Indigenous languages

The Book of Common Prayer has also been translated into these North American indigenous languages: Cowitchan, Cree, Haida, Ntlakyapamuk, Slavey, Eskimo-Aleut, Dakota, Delaware, Mohawk, Ojibwe.[5]

Ojibwa

Joseph Gilfillan was the chief editor of the 1911 Ojibwa edition of the Book of Common Prayer entitled *Iu Wejibuewisi Mamawi Anamiawini Mazinaigun* (*Iw Wejibwewizi Maamawi-anami'aawini Mazina'igan*) .

United States

The Episcopal Church separated itself from the Church of England in 1789, having been established in the United States in 1607. Its prayer book, published in 1790, had as its sources, the 1662 English book and the 1764 Scottish Liturgy (see above) which Bishop Seabury of Connecticut had brought over following his consecration in Aberdeen in 1784, containing elements of each . The preface to the 1789 Book of Common Prayer says "this Church is far from intending to depart from the Church of England in any essential point of doctrine, discipline, or worship...further than local circumstances require." There were some notable differences. For example, in the Communion service after the words of institution there follows a Prayer of Oblation from 1549, but into which were inserted the words 'which we now offer unto thee' (in small caps) with reference to the 'holy gifts'. An epiclesis was included, as in the Scottish book, though modified to meet reformist objections. Overall the book was modelled in the English Prayer Book, the Convention having resisted attempts at deletion and revision .

Further revisions occurred in 1892 and 1928, in which minor changes were made, removing, for instance, some of Cranmer's Exhortations and introducing such innovations as prayers for the dead.

In 1979, a more substantial revision was made. There were now two rites for the most common services, the first that kept most of the language of 1928, and the second using only contemporary language (some of it newly composed, and some adapted from the older language). Many changes were made in the rubrics and the shapes of the services, which were generally made for both the traditional and contemporary language versions. However, there was arguably a greater degree of continuity than was the case in England, which may account for the fact that all the books of the series, from 1790 to 1979 retain the same title. The 1979 book owes a good deal to the Liturgical Movement and to the 19th century Catholic revival. Many traditionalists, both Anglo-Catholics and Evangelicals, felt alienated by the theological changes made in the 1979 BCP, and in 1991 The Church of the Good Shepherd in

Rosemont, PA published a book entitled, the *Anglican Service Book* which is "a traditional language adaptation of the 1979 Book of Common Prayer together with the Psalter or Psalms of David and Additional Devotions." Books like this are allowed in the Episcopal Church because of a rubric in the 1979 Prayer Book which allows for the translation of the contemporary language into the traditional language of the 1928 Book of Common Prayer.

Even so, the revision caused some controversy and in 2000, the General Convention of the Episcopal Church issued an apology to those "offended or alienated during the time of liturgical transition to the 1979 Book of Common Prayer." Use of the 1928 Book of Common Prayer is currently discouraged. Article X of the Canons of the Episcopal Church provides that "[t]he Book of Common Prayer, as now established or hereafter amended by the authority of this Church, shall be in use in all the Dioceses of this Church," which, of course, is a reference to the 1979 Book of Common Prayer, but many parishes[6] still use it either regularly or occasionally, for pastoral sensitivity, for doctrinal reasons and for the beauty of its language.

The Prayer Book Cross was erected in San Francisco's Golden Gate Park in 1894 as a gift from the Church of England.[7] Created by Ernest Coxhead, it stands on one of the higher points in Golden Gate Park. It is located between John F. Kennedy Drive and Park Presidio Drive, near Cross Over Drive. This 57 ft (m) sandstone cross commemorates the first use of the Book of Common Prayer in California by Sir Francis Drake's chaplain on June 24, 1579.

Religious influence

The *Book of Common Prayer* has had a great influence on a number of other denominations. While theologically different, the language and flow of the service of many other churches owes a great debt to the prayer book. In particular, many Christian prayer books have drawn on the Collects for the Sundays of the Churches Year—mostly freely translated or even "rethought" by Cranmer from a wide range of Christian traditions, but including a number of original compositions—which are widely recognized as masterpieces of compressed liturgical construction.

John Wesley, an Anglican priest whose revivalist preaching led to the creation of Methodism wrote, "I believe there is no Liturgy in the world, either in ancient or modern language, which breathes more of a solid, scriptural, rational piety than the Common Prayer of the Church of England." Many Methodist churches in England and the United States continued to use a slightly revised version of the book for communion services well into the 20th century. In the United Methodist Church, the liturgy for Eucharistic celebrations is almost identical to what is found in the Book of Common Prayer, as are some of the other liturgies and services.

A unique variant was developed in 1785 in Boston, Massachusetts when the historic King's Chapel (founded 1686) left the Episcopal Church and became an independent Unitarian church. To this day, King's Chapel uniquely uses *The Book of Common Prayer According to the Use in King's Chapel* in its worship.

Literary influence

Together with the Authorized version and the works of Shakespeare, the Book of Common Prayer has been one of the three fundamental underpinnings of modern English. As it has been in regular use for centuries, many phrases from its services have passed into the English language, either as deliberate quotations or as unconscious borrowings. They are used in non-liturgical ways. For example, many authors have used quotes from the prayer book as titles for their books.

Some examples of well-known phrases from the Book of Common Prayer are:

- "Speak now or forever hold your peace" from the marriage liturgy.
- "Till death us do part", from the marriage liturgy.
- "Earth to earth, ashes to ashes, dust to dust" from the funeral service.
- "From all the deceits of the world, the flesh, and the devil" from the litany.
- "Read, mark, learn, and inwardly digest" from the collect for the second Sunday of Advent.

- "Evil liver" from the rubrics for Holy Communion.
- "All sorts and conditions of men" from the Order for Morning Prayer.
- "Peace in our time" from Morning Prayer, Versicles.

The phrase "till death us do part" ("till death us depart" before 1662[8]) has been changed to "till death do us part" in some more recent prayer books, such as the 1962 Canadian Book of Common Prayer.

References and allusions to Prayer Book services in the works of Shakespeare were tracked down and identified by Richmond Noble . Derision of the Prayer Book or its contents "in any interludes, plays, songs, rhymes, or by other open words" was a criminal offence under the 1559 Act of Uniformity,[9] and consequently Shakespeare avoids too direct reference; but Noble particularly identifies the reading of the Psalter according to the Great Bible version specified in the Prayer Book, as the biblical book generating the largest number of Biblical references in Shakespeare's plays. Noble found a total of 157 allusions to the Psalms in the plays of the First Folio, relating to 62 separate Psalms—all, save one, of which he linked to the version in the Psalter, rather than those in the Geneva Bible or Bishops' Bible. In addition, there are a small number of direct allusions to liturgical texts in the Prayer Book; e.g. Henry VIII 3:2 where Wolsey states "Vain Pomp and Glory of this World, I hate ye!", a clear reference to the rite of Public Baptism; where the Godparents are asked "Doest thou forsake the vaine pompe and glory of the worlde..?"

More recently, P.D. James used phrases from the *Book of Common Prayer* and made them into bestselling titles—*Devices and Desires* and *The Children of Men,* while Alfonso Cuarón's 2006 film *Children of Men* placed the phrase onto cinema marquees worldwide.

Copyright status

As the Book of Common Prayer is long out of copyright, it can be freely reproduced in most of the world. However, in the United Kingdom, the Crown holds the rights as part of the royal prerogative and as such, they are perpetual. Publishers are licensed to reproduce the Book of Common Prayer under letters patent which prohibit anyone other than the holders (and those authorized by them) from printing, publishing or importing the Book of Common Prayer into the United Kingdom.

Letters patent for England, Wales and Northern Ireland are held by the Queen's Printer, and for Scotland by the Scottish Bible [10] Board. The office of Queen's Printer has been associated with the right to reproduce the Bible for many years, with the earliest known reference coming in 1577. Other letters patent of similar antiquity grant Cambridge University Press and Oxford University Press the right to produce the Book of Common Prayer independently of the Queen's Printer. The Queen's Printer is currently the Cambridge University Press as from their takover of Eyre & Spottiswoode (which had been Queen's Printer since 1901) in the late 20th century. The protection that the Book of Common Prayer and the Authorized Version enjoy is the last remnant of the time when the Crown held a monopoly over all printing and publishing in the United Kingdom. This prerogative should not be confused with Crown copyright, or copyright in works of the United Kingdom's government.

The Episcopal Church's book is always released into the public domain.[11] Trial use and supplemental liturgies are however copyrighted by Church Publishing, the official publishing arm of the church.

See also

- Anglican devotions
- Book of Common Order
- Prayer Book Rebellion
- Prayer Book Society of Canada
- The Homilies
- Thirty-Nine Articles

Editions

- Anglican Church of Canada (1964). *The Canadian Book of Occasional Offices: Services for Certain Occasions not Provided in the Book of Common Prayer*, compiled by the Most Rev. Harold E. Sexton, Abp. of British Columbia, published at the request of the House of Bishops of the Anglican Church of Canada. Toronto: Anglican Church of Canada, Dept. of Religious Education. x, 162 p.
- Anglican Catholic Church of Canada (198-?). *When Ye Pray: Praying with the Church*, [by] Roland F. Palmer [an editor of the 1959/1962 Canadian B.C.P.]. Ottawa: Anglican Catholic Convent Society. *N.B.*: "This book is a companion to the Prayer Book to help ... to use the Prayer Book better."—Pg. 1. Without ISBN
- Reformed Episcopal Church in Canada and Newfoundland (1892). *The Book of Common Prayer and Administration of the Sacraments and Other Rites and Ceremonies of the Church, According to the Use of the Reformed Episcopal Church in the Dominion of Canada, Otherwise Known as the Protestant Church of England....* Toronto, Ont.: Printed ... by the Ryerson Press ... for the Synod of Canada, 1951, t.p. verso 1892. *N.B.*: This is the liturgy as it had been authorized in 1891.
- Church in Wales (1984). *The Book of Common Prayer, for the Use in the Church in Wales*. Penarth, Wales: Church in Wales Publications. 2 vol. *N.B.*: Title also in Welsh on vol. 2: *Y Llfr Gweddi Giffredin i'w arfer yn Yr Eglwys yng Nghymru*; vol. 1 is entirely in English; vol. 2 is in Welsh and English on facing pages. Without ISBN
- The Episcopal Church (2003). *The Book of Common Prayer: Selected Liturgies ... According to the Use of the Episcopal Church = Le Livre de la prière commune: Liturgies sélectionnées ... selon l'usage de l'Eglise Épiscopale*. Paris: Convocation of American Churches in Europe. 373, [5] p. *N.B.*: Texts in English and as translated into French, from the 1979 B.C.P. of the Episcopal Church (U.S.A.), on facing pages. ISBN 0-89869-448-5
- Reformed Episcopal Church (U.S.A.)(1932). The *Book of Common Prayer, According to the Use of the Reformed Episcopal Church in the United States of America*. Rev. fifth ed. Philadelphia, Penn.: Reformed Episcopal Publication Society, 1963, t.p. 1932. xxx, 578 p. *N.B.*: On p. iii: "[T]he revisions made ... in the Fifth Edition [of 1932] are those authorized by the [Reformed Episcopal] General Councils from 1943 through 1963."

Notes

Extended Note

[1] Widely varying figures are quoted. Procter and Frere (1902) gave 2000; Neill (1960, p. 165),1760. Spurr gives the following breakdown for the period 1660–63: Total ministers forced out of English parishes about 1760. This includes 695 parish ministers ejected under the 1660 act for settling clergy; 936 more forced out under the 1662 Act of Uniformity. In addition 200 non-parochial ministers from lectureships, universities and schools, and 120 in Wales were excluded. He adds that 171 of the 1760 are "known to have conformed later". In a footnote he cites Pruett (1978, p. 17,18,23).

[2] http://justus.anglican.org/resources/bcp/Muss-Arnolt/ch7&8.htm

[4] According to the Tables of Proper Psalms (http://www.prayerbook.ca/bcp/psalmstables.html), "The following passages in the Psalter as hitherto used are omitted: Psalm 14. 5-7; 55. 16; 58 (all); 68. 21-23; 69. 23-29; 104. 35 (in part); 109. 5-19; 136. 27; 137. 7-9; 140. 9-10; 141. 7-8. The verses are renumbered." See also the Psalter from 1962 Canadian Book of Common Prayer (http://www.prayerbook.ca/bcp/psalter.html).

[6] http://pbsusa.org/PBLinks.htm

[7] Prayer Book Cross (http://www.lightight.com/GGP/mem_images/Mem3P02.html)

[8] James E. Clapp, "till death us do part," (http://www.randomhouse.com/wotd/?date=20001013) The Mavens' Word of the Day (October 13, 2000).
[9] Act of Uniformity, 1559 (http://members.shaw.ca/reformation/1559uniformity.htm)
[10] http://www.scottishbiblesociety.org
[11] Canon II.3.6(b)(2) (http://www.churchpublishing.org/general_convention/pdf_const_2006/Title_II_Worship.pdf)

Other Notes

References

- Lewis, C.S. (196-). *"Miserable Offenders": an Interpretation of [sinfulness and] Prayer Book Language [about it],* in series, *The Advent Papers*. Cincinnati, Ohio: Forward Movement Publications.

Further reading

Chronological order of publication (oldest first):

- Forbes, Dennis (1992). Did the Almighty intend His book to be copyrighted?, *European Christian Bookstore Journal*, April 1992

External links

- Books of Common Prayer (http://justus.anglican.org/resources/bcp/), from various Provinces of the Anglican Communion, curated by Charles Wohlers at Society of Archbishop Justus.
- The Prayer Book Society (UK) (http://www.pbs.org.uk)

Act_of_Parliament

An **Act of Parliament** is a statute (commonly and mistakenly called a law) enacted as primary legislation by a national or sub-national parliament. In the Republic of Ireland the term Act of the Oireachtas is used, and in the United States the term Act of Congress is used.

In Commonwealth countries, the term is used both in a narrow sense, as the formal description of a law passed in certain territories, and in a wider (generic) sense for primary legislation passed in any country.

Bills

A draft Act of Parliament is known as a bill.

In territories with a Westminster system, most bills that have any possibility of becoming law are introduced into parliament by the government. This will usually happen following the publication of a "white paper", setting out the issues and the way in which the proposed new law is intended to deal with them. A bill may also be introduced into parliament without formal government backing; this is known as a private member's bill.

In territories with a multicameral parliament, most bills may be first introduced in any chamber. However, certain types of legislation are required, either by constitutional convention or by law, to be introduced into a specific chamber. For example, bills imposing a tax, or involving public expenditure, are introduced into the House of Commons in the United Kingdom by convention, and in Canada's House of Commons and Ireland's Dáil as a matter of law. Conversely, bills proposed by the Law Commission and consolidation bills traditionally start in the House of Lords.

Once introduced, a bill must go through a number of stages before it can become law. In theory, this allows the bill's provisions to be debated in detail, and for amendments to the original bill to also be introduced, debated, and agreed to.

In bicameral parliaments, a bill that has been approved by the chamber into which it was introduced then "sends" the bill to the other chamber. Broadly speaking, each chamber must separately agree to the same version of the bill. Finally, the approved bill receives assent; in most territories this is merely a formality, and is often a function exercised by the head of state.

In some countries, such as in Spain and Portugal, the term for a bill differs depending on whether it is initiated by the government (when it is known as a "project"), or by the Parliament (a "proposition", i.e., a private member's bill).

Procedure

Australia

In Australia, the bill passes through the following stages:

1. First reading: This stage is a mere formality.
2. Second reading: As in the UK, the stage involves a debate on the general principles of the bill and is followed by a vote. Again, the second reading of a Government bill is usually approved. A defeat for a Government bill on this reading signifies a major loss. If the bill is read a second time, it is then considered in detail
3. Consideration in detail: This usually takes place on the floor of the House. Generally, committees sit on the floor of the House and consider the bill in detail.
4. Third reading: A debate on the final text of the bill, as amended. Very rarely do debates occur during this stage.
5. Passage: The bill is then sent to the other House (to the Senate, if it originated in the House of Representatives; to the House of Representatives, if it is a Senate bill), which may amend it. If the other House amends the bill, the bill and amendments are posted back to the original House for a further stage. The State of Queensland's Parliament is unicameral and skips this and the rest of the stages.
6. Consideration of Senate/Representatives amendments: The House in which the bill originated considers the amendments made in the other House. It may agree to them, amend them, propose other amendments in lieu, or reject them. However, the Senate may not amend money bills, though it can "request" the House to make amendments. A bill may pass backwards and forwards several times at this stage, as each House amends or rejects changes proposed by the other. If each House insists on disagreeing with the other, the Bill is lost.
7. Disagreement between the Houses: Often, when a bill cannot be passed in the same form by both Houses, it is "laid aside", i.e. abandoned. There is also a special constitutional procedure allowing the passage of the bill without the separate agreement of both houses. If the House twice passes the same bill, and the Senate twice fails to pass that bill (either through rejection or through the passage of unacceptable amendments), then the Governor-General may dissolve both Houses of Parliament simultaneously and call an election for the entire Parliament. This is called a double dissolution. After the election, if the House again passes the bill, but the deadlock between the Houses persists, then the Governor-General may convene a joint sitting of both Houses, where a final decision will be taken on the bill. Although the House and the Senate sit as a single body, bills passed at a joint sitting are treated as if they had been passed by each chamber separately. The procedure only applies if the bill originated in the House of Representatives. Six double dissolutions have occurred, though a joint sitting was only held once, in 1974.
8. The bill is sent to the viceroy (the Governor-General for the Commonwealth and the ACT; the Governor for a State; the Administrator for a Territory) for the Royal Assent. Certain bills must be reserved by the viceroy for the Queen's personal assent.

Canada

In Canada, the bill passes through the following stages:

1. First reading: This stage is a mere formality.
2. Second reading: As in the UK, the stage involves a debate on the general principles of the bill and is followed by a vote. Again, the second reading of a government bill is usually approved. A defeat for a Government bill on this reading signifies a major loss. If the bill is read a second time, then it progresses to the committee stage.
3. Committee stage: This usually takes place in a standing committee of the Commons or Senate.
   - Standing committee: The standing committee is a permanent one; each committee deals with bills in specific subject areas. Canada's standing committees are similar to the UK's select committees.
   - Special committee: A committee established for a particular purpose, be it the examination of a bill or a particular issue.
   - Legislative committee: Similar to a special committee in that it is established for the consideration of a particular bill. The chairmanship is determined by the Speaker, rather than elected by the members of the committee. Not used in the Senate.
   - Committee of the Whole: The whole house sits as a committee in the House of Commons or Senate. Most often used to consider appropriation bills, but can be used to consider any bill.

   The committee considers each clause of the bill, and may make amendments to it. Significant amendments may be made at committee stage. In some cases, whole groups of clauses are inserted or removed. However, if the Government holds a majority, almost all the amendments which are agreed to in committee will have been tabled by the Government to correct deficiencies in the bill or to enact changes to policy made since the bill was introduced (or, in some cases, to import material which was not ready when the bill was presented).
4. Report stage: this takes place on the floor of the appropriate chamber, and allows the House or Senate to approve amendments made in committee, or to propose new ones.
5. Third reading: A debate on the final text of the bill, as amended.
6. Passage: The bill is then sent to the other House (to the Senate, if it originated in the House of Commons; to the Commons, if it is a Senate bill), where it will face a virtually identical process. If the other House amends the bill, the bill and amendments are sent back to the original House for a further stage.
7. Consideration of Senate/Commons amendments: The House in which the bill originated considers the amendments made in the other House. It may agree to them, amend them, propose other amendments in lieu or reject them. If each House insists on disagreeing with the other, the Bill is lost.
8. Disagreement between the Houses: There is no specific procedure under which the Senate's disagreement can be overruled by the Commons. The Senate's rejection is absolute.

The debate on each stage is actually debate on a specific motion. For the first reading, there is no debate. For the second reading, the motion is "That this bill be now read a second time and be referred to [name of committee]" and for third reading "That this bill be now read a third time and pass." In the Committee stage, each clause is called and motions for amendments to these clauses, or that the clause stand part of the bill are made. In the Report stage, the debate is on the motions for specific amendments.

Once a bill has passed both Houses in an identical form, it receives final, formal examination by the Governor General who gives it the Royal Assent. Although the Governor General can refuse to assent a bill or reserve the bill for the Queen at this stage, this power has never been exercised.

Bills being reviewed by Parliament are assigned numbers: 2 to 200 for government bills, 201 to 1000 for private member's bills, and 1001 up for private bills. They are preceded by C- if they originate in the House of Commons, or S- if they originate in the Senate. For example, Bill C-250 was a private member's bill introduced in the House. Bills C-1 and S-1 are pro forma bills, and are introduced at the beginning of each session in order to assert the right of each Chamber to manage its own affairs. They are introduced and read a first time, and then are dropped from the

Order Paper.

New Zealand

In New Zealand, the bill passes through the following stages:

1. First reading: MPs debate and vote on the bill. If a bill is approved, it passes on to the committee stage.
2. Select committee stage: The bill is considered by a Select Committee, which scrutinises the bill in detail and hears public submissions on the matter. The Committee may recommend amendments to the bill.
3. Second reading: The general principles of the bill are debated, and a vote is held. If the bill is approved, it is put before a Committee of the House.
4. Committee of the House: The bill is debated and voted on, clause by clause, by the whole House sitting as a committee.
5. Third reading: Summarising arguments are made, and a final vote is taken. If the bill is approved, it is passed to the Governor-General for Royal Assent. New Zealand has no upper house, and so no approval is necessary.

United Kingdom

United Kingdom Parliament

A draft piece of legislation is called a *bill*, when this is passed by Parliament it becomes an *Act* and part of statute law. There are two types of bill and Act, *public* and *private*. Public Acts apply to the whole of the UK or a number of its constituent countries — England, Scotland, Wales and Northern Ireland. Private Acts are local and personal in their effect, giving special powers to bodies such as local authorities or making exceptions to the law in particular geographic areas.[1]

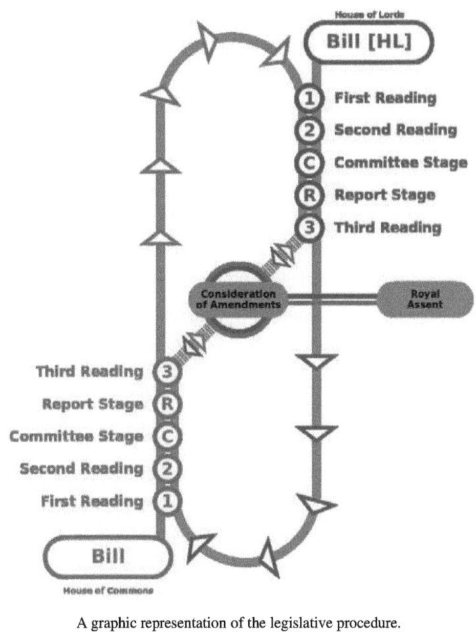

A graphic representation of the legislative procedure.

In the United Kingdom Parliament, each bill passes through the following stages:

1. Pre-legislative scrutiny: Not undertaken for all bills; usually a joint committee of both houses will review a bill and vote on amendments that the government can either accept or reject. The report from this stage can be influential in later stages as rejected recommendations from the committee are revived to be voted on.
2. First reading: This is a formality; no vote occurs. The Bill is presented and ordered to be printed and, in the case of private members' bills, a date is set for second reading.
3. Second reading: A debate on the general principles of the bill is followed by a vote.
4. Committee stage: This usually takes place in a public bill committee in the Commons and on the Floor of the House in the Lords. The committee considers each clause of the bill, and may make amendments to it.
5. Consideration (or report) stage: this takes place on the floor of the House, and is a further opportunity to amend the bill. Unlike committee stage, the House need not consider every clause of the bill, only those to which

amendments have been tabled.

6. Third reading: a debate on the final text of the bill, as amended in the House of Lords. Further amendments may be tabled at this stage.
7. Passage: The bill is then sent to the other House (to the Lords, if it originated in the Commons; to the Commons, if it is a Lords bill), which may amend it.
8. Consideration of Lords/Commons amendments: The House in which the bill originated considers the amendments made in the other House.
9. Royal assent.

Scottish Parliament

In the Scottish Parliament, bills pass through the following stages:

1. Introduction: The Bill is introduced to the Parliament together with its accompanying documents — Explanatory Notes, a Policy Memorandum setting out the policy underlying the Bill and a Financial Memorandum setting out the costs and savings associated with it. Statements from the Presiding Officer and the member in charge of the Bill are also lodged, indicating whether the Bill is within the legislative competence of the Parliament.
2. Stage one: The Bill is considered by one or more of the subject Committees of the Parliament, which normally take evidence from the bill's promoter and other interested parties before reporting to the Parliament on the principles of the Bill. Other Committees, notably the Finance and Subordinate Legislation Committees, may also feed in at this stage. The report from the Committee is followed by a debate in the full Parliament.
3. Stage two: The Bill returns to the subject Committee where it is subject to line-by-line scrutiny and amendment. This is similar to the Committee Stage in the UK Parliament.
4. Stage three: The Bill as amended by the Committee returns to the full Parliament. There is a further opportunity for amendment, followed by a debate on the whole Bill, at the end of which the Parliament decides whether to pass the Bill.
5. Royal assent: After the Bill has been passed, the Presiding Officer submits it to Her Majesty for Royal Assent. However he cannot do so until a 4-week period has elapsed during which the Law Officers of the Scottish Executive or UK Government can refer the Bill to the Supreme Court of the United Kingdom for a ruling on whether the Bill is within the powers of the Parliament.

There are special procedures for emergency bills, member's bills (similar to private member's bills in the UK Parliament), committee bills, and private bills.

Singapore

In Singapore, the bill passes through these certain stages before becoming into an Act of Parliament.

1. First Reading: The bill is introduced to the government, usually by the members of parliament. The unicameral parliament will then discuss the bill, followed by a vote. Voting must be at least 1/2 aye for non-controversial bills and 2/3 aye for controversial ones. If the bill passes the vote it will proceed to the second reading.
2. Second Reading: In this stage, the bill is further discussed and put to a second vote. If more than half of the votes are aye the bill proceeds to the select committee.
3. Select Committee: The select committee consists of people not only from the parliaments, but also the people who could be affected by the bill is passed into law. This is to ensure equity and that the bill is fair for all. If the Bill is in favor, it will proceed to the third reading.
4. Third Reading: After the select committee has discussed and are in favor of the bill, they will put it to a vote. At this juncture, if the votes are more than 1/2 aye, it will be sent to the President of Singapore, currently Tony Tan. This is known as President Assent.
5. President Assent: The president must give permission in order for the bill to be passed. If he approves it, it will become a statute passed down by the members of parliament which is called an Act of Parliament.

Titles and citation of Acts

Acts passed by the Parliament of England did not originally have titles, and could only be formally cited by reference to the parliamentary session in which they were passed, with each individual Act being identified by a chapter number. Descriptive titles began to be added to the enrolled Acts by the official clerks, as a reference aid; over time, titles came to be included within the text of each bill. Since the mid-nineteenth century, it has also become common practice for Acts to have a short title, as a convenient alternative to the sometimes lengthy main titles.

The numerical citation of Acts has also changed over time. The original method was based on the regnal year(s) in which the relevant parliament session met. This has been replaced in most territories by simple reference to the calendar year, with the first Act passed being chapter 1, and so on.

Until the 1980s, Acts of the Australian state of Victoria were numbered in a continuous sequence from 1857; thus the Age of Majority Act 1977 was No. 9075 of 1977.

See also

- Act of Congress
- Legislative act
- Halsbury's Statutes
- List of Acts of Parliament in the United Kingdom
- Table of contents

References

[1] p. 190, *How Parliament Works*, 6th edition, Robert Rogers and Rhodri Walters, Pearson Longman, 2006

- www.publications.parliament.uk (http://www.publications.parliament.uk/pa/ld/ldcomp/ldctso26.htm)

External links

- All Acts of Parliament (since 1988) and statutory instruments are available free on-line under Crown copyright terms from the Office of Public Sector Information (OPSI (http://www.opsi.gov.uk/)).
- Acts of Parliament (since 1267) revised to date are available free on-line under Crown copyright terms from the Ministry of Justice (SLD (http://www.statutelaw.gov.uk/)).
- Parliamentary Stages of a Government Bill (pdf) (http://www.parliament.uk/documents/upload/l01.pdf) from the House of Commons Information Office.
- Acts of the Commonwealth Parliament of Australia: ComLaw.gov.au (http://www.comlaw.gov.au/Browse/ByYearNumber/Acts/Historical/0/0/)

Burial_Laws_Amendment_Act_1880

The Burial Laws Amendment Act 1880 (43 & 44 Vict c 41) is an Act of the Parliament of the United Kingdom. It is one of the Burial Acts 1852 to 1885.[1]

This Act is excluded by section 4 [2] of the Welsh Church (Burial Grounds) Act 1945.

For the construction of references in this Act to a "parish" or "burial board", in the application of this Act to Greater London, see section 44(4) [3] of the London Government Act 1963.

From 1882 to 1961, this Act was applied by section 3 of the Interments (felo de se) Act 1882.

Preamble

The preamble was repealed by the Statute Law Revision Act 1894.

Section 7 - Burials to be conducted in a decent and orderly manner and without obstruction

This section reads:

> All burials under this Act, whether with or without a religious service, shall be conducted in a decent and orderly manner; and every person guilty of any riotous, violent, or indecent behaviour at any burial under this Act, or wilfully obstructing such burial or any such service as aforesaid thereat, or who shall, in any such churchyard or graveyard as aforesaid, deliver any address, not being part of or incidental to a religious service permitted by this Act, and not otherwise permitted by any lawful authority, or who shall, under colour of any religious service or otherwise, in any such churchyard or graveyard, wilfully endeavour to bring into contempt or obloquy the Christian religion, or the belief or worship of any church or denomination of Christians, or the members or any minister of any such church or denomination, or any other person, shall be guilty of a misdemeanor.[4]

"Riotous"

See sections 10(3) and (4) of the Public Order Act 1986.

Sentence

A person guilty of this offence is liable to imprisonment for a term not exceeding two years.[5]

Where a person is convicted on indictment of this offence, the court, if not precluded from sentencing an offender by its exercise of some other power, may impose a fine instead of or in addition to dealing with him in any other way in which the court has power to deal with him, subject however to any enactment requiring the offender to be dealt with in a particular way.[6]

Proposal for repeal

In 1985, the Law Commission said that this offence was no longer used and recommended that it be repealed.[7]

In 1981, they said that in relation to cemeteries and crematoria managed by local authorities, this offence was effectively superseded by articles 18 and 19 of the Local Authorities' Cemeteries Order 1977 (SI 1977/204), made under section 214 of the Local Government Act 1972.[8] They also said that there was a considerable overlap with the offence in section 2 of the Ecclesiastical Courts Jurisdiction Act 1860.[9]

Section 11 - Order of coroner or certificate of registrar to be delivered to relative, etc instead of to person who buries

This section was repealed by section 13(1) [10] of, and Second Schedule [11] to, the Births and Deaths Registration Act 1926.

References

- Halsbury's Statutes,

[1] The Short Titles Act 1896, section 2(1) and Schedule 2
[2] http://www.legislation.gov.uk/ukpga/Geo6/8-9/27/section/4
[3] http://www.legislation.gov.uk/ukpga/1963/33/section/44
[4] Digitised copy of section 7 (http://www.legislation.gov.uk/ukpga/Vict/43-44/41/section/7) from Legislation.gov.uk
[5] Castro v R (1880) 5 QBD 490 at 508; the Powers of Criminal Courts (Sentencing) Act 2000, section 77 (http://www.legislation.gov.uk/ukpga/2000/6/section/77)
[6] The Criminal Justice Act 2003, section 163 (http://www.legislation.gov.uk/ukpga/2003/44/section/163)
[7] The Law Commission. Criminal Law: Offences against Religion and Public Worship. Law Com 145. HMSO. London. 1985. Paragraph 3.25 at page 39.
[8] The Law Commission. Offences against Religion and Public Worship. Working Paper No 79. HMSO. London. 1981. Paragraphs 12.11 and 12.21 at pages 152 and 160.
[9] The Law Commission. Offences against Religion and Public Worship. Working Paper No 79. HMSO. London. 1981. Paragraph 12.13 at page 154.
[10] http://www.legislation.gov.uk/ukpga/Geo5/16-17/48/section/13/enacted
[11] http://www.legislation.gov.uk/ukpga/Geo5/16-17/48/schedule/SECOND/enacted

External links

- The Burial Laws Amendment Act 1880 (http://www.legislation.gov.uk/ukpga/Vict/43-44/41/contents), as amended from the National Archives.
- The Burial Laws Amendment Act 1880 (http://www.legislation.gov.uk/ukpga/Vict/43-44/41/contents/enacted), as originally enacted from the National Archives.

Article Sources and Contributors

Act_of_Uniformity_Amendment_Act_1872 *Source*: http://en.wikipedia.org/w/index.php?title=Act_of_Uniformity_Amendment_Act_1872 *Contributors*: Bearcat, John of Reading, Katharineamy, Qetuth, Rumping, Tim!

Parliament_of_the_United_Kingdom *Source*: http://en.wikipedia.org/w/index.php?title=Parliament_of_the_United_Kingdom *Contributors*: 2toise, A.K.A.47, ABF, AHM, AJR, Aaron7chicago, AaronSw, Aaronjbaylis, Acanon, Adam Bishop, AdamBMorgan, Addup2, Ahoerstemeier, Alansohn, Alex, Alkari, Alkivar, Amakuru, Amunra reborn, Analogdrift, Andrew Gray, Andrew Gwilliam, Andrew L (2005), Andrew Yong, Andy120290, Andypandy.UK, Angusmclellan, Antandrus, Anthony, Aquarius Rising, Aricci526, Arpingstone, Arthur Holland, Aspects, Average Earthman, Axl, Axxgreazz, BD2412, Banjee ca, Barryob, Barticus88, BasilSorbie, Bastique, Bdb484, Beardo, Bencherlite, Betacommand, Bhadani, BilCat, BillC, Billreid, Birdhurst, Blueflavouredcat, Bobblewik, Bobdylanlol, Bodnotbod, Boing! said Zebedee, Bojette, Bornintheguz, Boson, Bouzouki500, Bovlb, Bradpogo, Braingle, BritishWatcher, BruceW07, Bsadowski1, Burto88, Cameron, Capricorn42, Cavrdg, Ccacsmss, Centrx, Chris Roy, Chrisieboy, Chrism, Clarince63, Clausule, Cloudbound, Coffee, Compfreak7, Computerjoe, Conversion script, Cosmo0, Croatnik, Csernica, CubistUterus, Curps, Cutler, Cybercobra, Cyberpower678, Cynical, D22, DVD R W, DabMachine, Daibhid C, Daicaregos, Dancing is Forbidden, Danio, Bibliophylax, Dannnny sdfhjkjhgrc bghrdc5434657, Dave souza, Daveboxley, David Newton, David the Aspie, DavidFarmbrough, Davidkinnen, Dendodge, Derek Ross, Deus Ex, Diliff, Discospinster, Dmvward, DocWatson42, Dom0803, DonBarton, Doops, Doortmont, Dpaajones, DrKiernan, Duffman, Duroy, ES Vic, ESkog, Eddore, Eixo, Eje211, Elagatis, ElationAviation, Electionworld, Enigmaman, Epbr123, EquecoLondon, Eraserhead1, Erud, Erudnetti, Escottf, Esrever, Etrigan, Eurosong, Evercat, Everyking, FClef, Facebookman123, Finlay McWalter, Fishiehelper2, Fornost, Francium12, Fratrep, Freemarket, Frietjes, Froggo Zijgeb, Fvw, Fys, G-Man, Gabbe, Gadfium, Gaius Cornelius, Galoubet, Gary J, Gene.arboit, Geo Swan, Georen9, George Burgess, Ghmyrtle, Glane23, Gold Wiz113, Good Olfactory, Gorrrillla5, Green01, Greenguy1090, Grimhelm, Ground Zero, Guyfawkes69, Gvotno, Gwernol, Hairy Dude, Haldraper, HalfShadow, Hammersfan, Hazhk, Hede2000, Henry Flower, Henrygb, Hermis, Heron, Heyman3, Hibernian, HighKing, Highground5, Hmains, Hoshie, Howard Alexander, Icairns, Ichwan Palongengi, Ikari, Illinoisavonlady, Infrogmation, Iota, Irshgrl500, JW1805, JaT, JackofOz, James500, James57, JamesMLane, Jamiemaloneyscoreg, Jammydodger, JasonAQuest, Jauhienij, Jay32183, Jayron32, Jazzwick, Jdforrester, Jecar, Jezzabr, Jfruh, Jhbdel, Jiang, Jjron, Johnbod, Johnleemk, Join now!, Jombo, Jon C., Joshua, Jtdirl, Jza84, K1210349, Kaihsu, Kalmalid, Kayman1uk, Kbthompson, Keith D, Keithgreer, Kimyestjolie, King brosby, Klausness, Koavf, Kungfuadam, Kurando, Lamberhurst, Laurel Bush, Laurens, Leandrod, LedgendGamer, Lemonade100, Lethbridge-Stewart, Lightmouse, Limideen, Linburats, Lionel Elie Mamane, Livitup, Lord Emsworth, Lordrosemount, Lotje, Lucy-marie, Lupin, MAG1, MRSC, Ma Baker, Maartenvdbent, Magnus Manske, Mais oui!, Manelbest, Mani1, Marcsin, Marcus Qwertyus, Marechal Ney, Marianika, Markjp99, Martg76, MartinHarper, Martynas Patasius, Matt1299, Mattissa, Mattmatt1987, Mauls, Mboverload, Merbabu, Merrybrit, Mic, Mikeplokta, Mikeyandreality, Mimihitam, Miniguy222, Mintguy, MisfitToys, Mitchitara, Mjarrar, Mm40, Mo ainm, Modest Genius, Montrealais, Moonraker, Moormand, Mooshoo88888, Morton dill, Morwen, Mr Taz, MrJones, Mutt Lunker, Muzi, Mxn, MykReeve, Ned Morrell, Neuralwarp, Neutrality, Newprogressive, Nickmundt, Nilmerg, Nomad2u001, Oerjan, Olegwiki, Osioni, Ouip, OwenBlacker, PBS, PBS-AWB, Pagw, Pajz, Panser Born, Panthro, Pat Payne, Patsfan021, Pauldanon, Peterkingiron, Pharillon, Pharos, Philip Stevens, Philip Trueman, Picus viridis, Pigman, Piotrus, Plek, Plucas58, Pluma, Pmyteh, Pol098, PrimeHunter, Proman1983, Proteus, QTCaptain, QatarStarsLeague, Quadell, QuartierLatin1968, Quindie, RMHED, Rbrwr, Rcbutcher, Realitybias, Reysolano100, Reywas92, Rich Farmbrough, Richard75, Richardguk, Rnt20, Road Wizard, Roadrunner, Roberdin, Robert Bond, Robinhw, Roeeyaron, Royslater999, Rrius, Rumping, Rupertslander, RuthCobb, Rutld001, SE7, SGBailey, Saga City, Sam Blacketer, Sam Hocevar, Sammyxxxxxx, Sander123, Sandy Scott, SandyGeorgia, Scolaire, Scottybowl, Selket, Sgt Pinback, ShelfSkewed, Shirulashem, Shoreranger, Simon Harley, Simon P Blackburn, SimonP, Slakr, Smb1001, Smelialichu, Sorter.Daniels, SouthernNights, Spannerdan, Springwalk, Srleffler, Ssolbergj, Steel, Steinsky, Stephen Kennedy, Stephennarmstrong, Stevietheman, Storm Rider, Str1977, Straw Cat, Stuz, Subin.a.mathew, Swid, Sylvain1972, TFMcQ, TaerkastUA, Tankerlator, Taxman, Tb, Tdslappy, TedE, Textorus, Tgsh2005, TharkunColl, The Anome, The C of E, The Duke of Waltham, The Thing That Should Not Be, The idiot, TheoClarke, ThinkingTwice, Thumperward, Tim Parenti, Tim!, TimR, Tktru, Tobias Conradi, Tobias Hoevekamp, Toddst1, Tom Edwards, Tommy2010, Tony Corsini, Tracield, Travis Cleveland, TreasuryTag, TreveX, Trm90, TrufflesTheLamb, TuaisceartÉireann, UK-Logician-2006, Ultra two, Vanerptimo2, Vanished user 5zariu3jisj0j4irj, Veledan, Verloren, Vilerage, Vostok412, Vrenator, Wabbit98, Wagnerp, Wally, Wbm1058, We hope, Welsh, Welshsocialist, Wereon, Widr, Woohookitty, Wooster, Wta121, Ww2censor, YankeeDoodle14, Yemen101, Zangar, Zigger, Zoney, Zundark, Zviki1, 212, Жељко Тодоровић, , 548 anonymous edits

Legislature *Source*: http://en.wikipedia.org/w/index.php?title=Legislature *Contributors*: 's-Gravenhage, 16@r, 2toise, 5 albert square, 72Dino, 8thstar, Accurizer, Addihockey10, Ahoerstemeier, Aitias, Ajhumph, Alansohn, Alex.muller, Alex756, Ali Esfandiari, Aliabdiali, Alinor, Allens, Altermike, Ameliorezquevous, Amondo, Andres, Aquarius Rising, Arctic-Editor, Arctic.gnome, Areth naar, Aricci526, Atlant, Avala, Avoided, Ayla, Backslash Forwardslash, Bagatelle, Barryob, Bastique, Battlesysadmin, Beast01659, Berland, Bfkerrigan, Bibowen, Big Bird, Big iron, Bjarki S, Bobble Hat, BobfromtheBeltway, Bonaparte, Bongwarrior, Borisblue, Branlon, BrianKnez, Brion VIBBER, Bumblebees1234, CWY2190, Cahk, Calmer Waters, Can't sleep, clown will eat me, CapitalR, Capricorn42, CatherineMunro, Cdw1952, Cfsenel, Choihei, Chrislk02, Chrism, Chun-hian, CieloEstrellado, Courcelles, Cpq29gpl, Crinoo, Cubs Fan, Cybercobra, Cyfex, D6, DRTllbrg, DVD R W, Da Vynci, Darth Panda, Dave6, Daven200520, Dcordobab, Deconstructhis, Delldot, Denelson83, Denlaw, DerHexer, Deror avi, Discospinster, Dmitri Yuriev, Docboat, Docu, Dogmom228, Download, Dreadstar, Drmies, Duffman, Dylan Lake, E.G., Earth, Eastlaw, Ed hover, Electionworld, Elm, Ember of Light, Epbr123, Eragon18, EugeneZelenko, Fanghong, FiggyBee, Firetrap9254, FlagSteward, Flewis, Fogster, Foochar, Francvs, Fred Bauder, Friedfish, Gaignun Kukai, Galoubet, Galteglise, Gareth Griffith-Jones, Garion96, Gauss, Gentgeen, Gillespe, Ginsengbomb, GoldRingChip, Goodnightmush, Gorillasapiens, GraemeL, Grampion76, Hafmark, Hammer1980, Hda3ku, Henriefa, Heracles31, Hersfold, Hghyux, Hiddekel, HighFlyingFish, Hmich176, Hut 8.5, I dream of horses, IRP, IngSoc BigBrother, Insanity Incarnate, Inspector 34, Instantnood, InverseHypercube, Iota, J.delanoy, Jacksonyguo, Jagun, JayJasper, Jayron32, Jeff G., Jengod, Jeterules, Jiang, Jim Douglas, Jim1138, Jj137, Jock Boy, JoeSmack, John254, JohnGH, Johnfuller99, Jojit fb, Jonathan321, JonathanDP81, Joy, Jpeob, Jrdioko, Jsteph, Jumbuck, Jurema Oliveira, Jusjih, KNewman, Ka Faraq Gatri, Kafziel, Keilana, Khendon, King of Hearts, Kingpin13, Knowledge-is-power, KnowledgeOfSelf, Knuckles, Koavf, Koumz, Kungfuadam, Kurt000, LOKIGaia, La Pianista, Lakers, Leafyplant, Legis, LizardJr8, Lmbstl, Lolcats2152, Lord Voldemort, Lost tourist, Lpgeffen, Ltwin, M.O.X, M3taphysical, M412k, MPerel, Majorly, Mallanox, Man It's So Loud In Here, Man vyi, Marek69, Mark Arsten, Martel,C, Martinkunev, Matthew Yeager, Maximus Rex, Mayooranathan, McSly, Mcornelius, Mic, Miles530, Mindspillage, Minna Sora no Shita, MisfitToys, Moe Epsilon, Montrealais, Morgankevinj, Mormegil, Morwen, Mr Gronk, MuZemike, Mudyy rox, Neo-Jay, Nighers Love You!!1, Nijusby, Nricardo, Nsalta, Nukeless, Nurtsio, Oxymoron83, PamD, Paste, PatriceNeff, Peterbr, Petri Krohn, Phantomsteve, Pharaoh of the Wizards, PhilKnight, Philip Trueman, Piano non troppo, Picapica, Pinethicket, Platewq, Polmandc, Portalian, Postdlf, PrincessSade, Producercunningham, ProfessorPaul, Pterodactyler, PullUpYourSocks, Quintote, R'n'B, RB972, Radon210, RainbowOfLight, Ramin1981, Rawling, RayneVanDunem, Rdsmith4, Reinhardheydt, Rickterp, Riyuky, Roadrunner, Robofish, RomanHistorian, RossPatterson, RoyBoy, RubleuleR, Ryan Postlethwaite, RyanCross, SMC, SPQRobin, Salampadpu, Sdggfhsdgy7237827, Seddon, Silivrenion, Singhalawap, Sionus, Slowking Man, Snickerdo, Snipesava, Snoyes, Some jerk on the Internet, Spinboy, Spitfire, Spoon!, SpyMagician, Squideshi, Station1, Steven Zhang, Stevietheman, Storm Rider, Studerby, Supersexyspacemonkey, SusikMkr, Syp, THEN WHO WAS PHONE?, Tanaats, Tanthalas39, Tedickey, Tejas81, Textangel, The Illusive Man, The Thing That Should Not Be, TheOriginalSoni, Thebestofall007, ThinkEnemies, Thirty-seven, Tide rolls, Tihanyi Joci, Tim!, Tohd8BohaithuGh1, Tommo 87, Tox, Treyt021, Triwbe, Tshase, Ttonyb1, UberScienceNerd, Unitmatrix01, Unschool, Utcursch, Vardion, Vino s, Waggers, Walden, Walshga, Wannabemodel, WatermelonPotion, WayeMason, Wayne Slam, Weien, Welsh, WhisperToMe, WikiTownsvillian, Wilfried Derksen, Wknight94, Wtshymanski, XJaM, Xanchester, Xivia1, Xp54321, Yamamoto Ichiro, Yst, ZX81, Zara-arush, Zigger, Zzyzx11, 890 anonymous edits

Parliament *Source*: http://en.wikipedia.org/w/index.php?title=Parliament *Contributors*: (, **FirstGenius**, 0lorenzo0, 2,4-dinitrophenylhydrazone, 207.17.47.xxx, 24.93.53.xxx, A suyash, A.Ou, A.h. king, A3RO, ABF, Abe Lincoln, Adam78, AdamM, Adammt23, Addlesee123456789, Addshore, AdjustShift, Agulvish, Ahmad87, Ahoerstemeier, Aitias, Ajgiddings, Ajk, Ajrs, Akamad, Alansohn, Aldog2k12, Aleenf1, Alex43223, AlexiusHoratius, AlfinIzraqsaatini, Alinor, Alison, Altermike, Altes, Amaury, Amire80, Anbu121, Andre Engels, Andrewman327, Andy120290, Angusmclellan, Anna512, Antandrus, Aoidh, Aoso0ck, Apparition11, Ares8, Arno, Arthena, Artoasis, Asterion, Astral, Avala, Az1568, Azkar, B Fizz, B. Meijlink, Bahar101, Banaticus, Bart Versieck, Beland, Bencherlite, Benjaminwhite31, Benji Franklyn, Benson85, BigDunc, Bigbang21, Biruitorul, Biscuit boy, Bkonrad, Black Kite, Blink484, Bob A, Bob Burkhardt, Bobharoldson, Bobo The Ninja, Bobo192, BokicaK, Boothy443, Bornintheguz, Breadandcheese, Brendandh, Briaboru, Brian the Editor, Brianann MacAmhlaidh, Bumcheeze, Bwilkins, Byrial, C mon, CARAVAGGISTI, CHJL, CK6569, CambridgeBayWeather, Capitalismojo, Capricorn42, CaribDigita, Catgut, Cdc, Cenarium, Cerian, Cescoby, Cflm001, Chanvis18, Chrism, Christopher Parham, ColdFusion200, Colonies Chris, CommonsDelinker, ConMan, Conversion script, Crazy Among, Csendesmark, Curps, Cyfal, D22, DARTH SIDIOUS 2, DabMachine, DaeX, Dan da man469, Danny-w, Danski14, David Newton, Dcordobab, Ddjc, Ddye, Deckiller, Deli nk, Delldot, Den fjättrade ankan, Deon, DerHexer, DeusMP, Devourer09, Dhakasumit2003, Digitalme, Dimimimon7, Discospinster, Djmutex, DocWatson42, Docu, Dogface, Donner60, E Wing, E.G., Earth, Eastfrisian, EdH, Edward, Edwy, Eesteren, Electionworld, Elmondo21st, Emperorbma, Emrrans, Energon, Erdeniss, Eric-Wester, Evbassboy13, Everyking, Fakeemcdontexist, Family Olofsson, Fastifex, FayssalF, Feedintm, Flewis, Forbes72, Fraggle81, Freakofnurture, Frehley, Frigotoni, FrstFrs, Furrykef, Gadren, Gaius Cornelius, Galoubet, GelatinDelight, Geschichte, Gfoley4, Giorgi sarukhanishvili, Glacialfox, Glane23, Gogo Dodo, Graham87, GregAsche, Ground Zero, Grutness, Gsjdgwey, Gwernol, Gzornenplatz, H.W., Harlanhaskins, Harlem Baker Hughes, Hbent, Hdt83, Headphonos, Hemlock Martinis, Henrygb, Hephaestos, HiLo48, HistoryBA, Hope with me, Htonl, Huaiwei, Humble-slave-patsy, Hurricanefan24, Hut 8.5, Huw Powell, Ian Pitchford, Iceflamer, Icseaturtles, Ifotography, Igoldste, Ihatetennis, Ikescs, Infocidal, Instantnood, Iota, Iretnas, Iridescent, Istvan, Ixfd64, J.delanoy, JJ Harrison, JaGa, Jack Greenmaven, Jagged 85, Jam420, James500, Jamespitts89, Jaxl, Jdforrester, JediKnight, Jespinos, JeuneJames, Jiang, Jinjoakhil, Jjhake, Joffeloff, John Price, John254, Johnleemk, Jose77, Joseph Solis in Australia, Jrleighton, Jrquinlisk, Jthomas123456789, Jutherine, Jwy, Kaihsu, Karl-Henner, Katieh5584, Kelly, King of Hearts (old account 2), Kingc, Kirbyiscottoncandy, Knight1993, Kralahome, Kudret abi, Kuru, Kuwaitsoccer, Lacrimosus, Lairor, Law Lord, Lazylaces, Leaf of Silver, Leemon2010, Lemonade100, Leujohn, Lightmouse, LightningProductions, Lizzie Harrison, Lollypopunk9526, Lugia2453, Luk, Luna Santin, Lupin, MC MasterChef, MNAdam, Mac, Madhero88, Magicalsaumy, Magnate, Mais oui!, Man vyi, Mark Malcampo, Martial75, Masamax, Matthew Fennell, Matthew Yeager, Maurice Carbonaro, Mav, Maxdillon, Maximaximax, McGeddon, Mclay1, Mdann52, Meatspin1, Mholland, Mic, Michael Hardy, Michaelpkk, Michiel Buddingh', Mighty Mighty Joe, MikeF9, Mnbf9rca, Montrealais, Moriori, Morwen, Moxy, Moyogo, Mr Gronk, MrRadrocker, Mrziggy1, MusikAnimal, MyNameWasTaken, NHRHS2010, NJackKaren, Nakon, Neelix, Neutrality, NewEnglandYankee, Niceguyedc, Noah Salzman, Nomad2u001, Normandy, NorthernThunder, Northgrove, Nyttend, O.Koslowski, Ohconfucius, Olivier, OpticalEnigma, Orbst, Ost316, Otto ter Haar, Oxymoron83, PBS-AWB, PIrish, Pandion auk, Patsfan021, Paul August, Pdcook, Peanut4, Phgao, Philip Stevens, Philip Trueman, Philippe Batreau, Picus viridis, Pmsyyz, Pogonomyrmex, Pointer1, Pooh-f-baby, Porges, Possum, Postdlf, Proman1983, Provocateur, Psbsub, Ptk, Puffin, Purplefire, Qelknap, Quadell, Quangbao, Qxz, R'n'B, Rago42, Rajakhr, Razorflame, Recurring dreams, RentAChemist, Retired username, Richard Arthur Norton (1958-), Richard75, Roadrunner, Robert Brockway, Roeeyaron, Rokbas, Romanm, Romanskolduns, Ronline, Rosiewoods35, Royalfalcon12, Ryan Heuser, Ryulong, SWAdair, Salam32, Sam Korn, SchfiftyThree, SchreiberBike, Schrödinger's Neurotoxin, Sciurinæ, Scottybowl, Scroggie, Seabhcan, Seattle Skier,

Sfgiants1995, ShelfSkewed, Shreshth91, Sietse Snel, Sikon, Sjakkalle, Sjorford, Sm8900, Smalljim, Smb1001, Smeggysmeg, SnowFire, Snowolf, Sodacan, SpLoT, Sparhawk08, Staeiou, Stephenb, Steven Zhang, Stevertigo, Sun Creator, Swid, Symane, Tabletop, Tanguin The Forager, Technopat, Technopilgrim, Teles, Tempodivalse, Ters, Teryx, Tgou, The Thing That Should Not Be, The Tom, The monkeyhate, The not fake mccoy, TheLetterM, Thhunter3, Thievinggypsy, Thirty-seven, Thisisbossi, Thrissel, Tillander, Tim boarding, Tim!, TimBentley, Tlonca, Tom Morris, Tombomp, Tomwalden, Tozznok, TravisM, Trevor MacInnis, Treybien, Twenex, Umar Zulfikar Khan, Uncle Dick, UnknownFork, Unpolloloco, Unused0029, Uriber, UtherSRG, VasilievVV, Velella, Velimir85, Verloren, Vicki Rosenzweig, Vipinhari, Vzbs34, Walden, Wayland, Webclient101, Wereon, Widr, Wiki Vendetta, Wiki alf, WikiDan61, Wikid77, Wilfried Derksen, Wimt, Witan, WmJHeart, WojPob, Woodstone, Woohookitty, Wpktsfs, X.xlovebugx.x, Xiahou, Xiaphias, Yellowdesk, Yvesnimmo, Zenohockey, Zirland, Zoppp, Zundark, Ævar Arnfjörð Bjarmason, لیقعق فشا, 844 anonymous edits

Book_of_Common_Prayer *Source*: http://en.wikipedia.org/w/index.php?title=Book_of_Common_Prayer *Contributors*: 1549bcp, ASK, Addedentry, Afterwriting, Alansplodge, Alexander Domanda, Andrew Yong, AndrewNJ, Andycjp, Anglicanus, Angr, Angusmclellan, AnnaKucsma, Balin42632003, Beardo, Beyond My Ken, Bhuck, Bitbut, Blaid, Bobblehead, Bonnenuitcher, Bradby, Brenont, Bryan Derksen, Bsadowski1, Cafemusique, Carandraug, Carolynparrishfan, Casper Gutman, Cassowary, Cgmusselman, Charles Matthews, Charleschuck, Cherubinirules, Chill doubt, Chmielok, Chowbok, ChrisGualtieri, Christopher W Rees, Circuitloss, Coemgenus, Conversion script, D Monack, DTOx, DVdm, Dabbler, DadaNeem, Dangerous-Boy, Danielsilliman, Dave souza, David Newton, David Underdown, Deuteronomist71, Dhixon1, DiiCinta, Dismas, Djnjwd, Domingo Portales, Don4of4, Dricherby, Dybryd, Easyer, Ehrenkater, Eliyak, Emargie, Engineer Bob, Felix Folio Secundus, Francispaulus, Frans Fowler, Frederick jones, GSTQ, Gabbe, Gaius Cornelius, Gary D, Garzo, Geogre, GreatWhiteNortherner, Greentubing, Grover cleveland, Gtg204y, Hackloon, Hoshie, Houtdsya, Hroðulf, Hymers2, I dream of horses, IkbenFrank, Impossiblename, Iridescent, Ironmaiden459, Itai, J R Gainey, J496, JW1805, Jamespeterka, Jdforrester, JesAceves, Jfhutson, Jiang, Jim1138, John Carter, John Paul Parks, Johnnybird, Josiah Rowe, Jpacobb, Jschnur, KHM03, Kathleen.wright5, Katiebearrbearr, Ken Gallager, Kibi78704, Kopaka649, LeBofSportif, Leandrod, Lightmouse, Ligulem, LilHelpa, Loringp, Lotje, Lucio Di Madaura, Magioladitis, Mais oui!, MakeRocketGoNow, MaliNorway, Man vyi, Mangoe, Manushand, Marcus Qwertyus, Masalai, Matilda, Metatron-777, Micjohn, Midnite Critic, Mikaellangner, Mike Christie, Mkopl98, NaGromOne, Nasugbu batangas, Nathanielfirst, Neddyseagoon, Nennius, Neo Ogilvy, Neutrality, Nrgdocadams, Nv8200p, Oknazevad, Ondewelle, One Salient Oversight, Orenburg1, PBSwiki, Palms99, Pcpcpc, Pcthoms, Peace2n4all, PeterGrecian, Pgg7, PhilHibbs, Philippe, Plasticup, Pseudo daoist, Ptolemy Caesarion, Pádraig Coogan, QVanillaQ, Quadell, Quintusdecimus, RBBrittain, Reedy, Reward, Rich Farmbrough, Richard75, Rjwilmsi, Rmhermen, Rockhopper10r, Roger Arguile, Rsquire3, Rursus, Rwflammang, SJK, Samw, Sbmackay, Scartol, Schizmatic, ShelleyAdams, Signalhead, Sirmylesnagopaleentheda, Sjorford, Smallbones, Smalljim, Smith2006, Subdeacon, Sun Creator, Surtsicna, Tahc, Tassedethe, Tb, Tcrichards, Ted Longstaffe, Terot, That Guy, From That Show!, The League of Crazy Men, Theopolisme, Timrollpickering, Toby Bartels, TomHennell, TopAce, Tristanb, Troyac, Tuckerresearch, Uberhill, Val1214, Vancouveriensis, Vanished user ewfisn2348tui2f8n2fio2utjfeoi210r39jf, Versus22, WRK, Waelsch, Wareh, Wassupwestcoast, Wikid77, Will Beback Auto, William Avery, Wolstan, Woohookitty, Wtmitchell, Xophist, YUL89YYZ, Yousou, Zenohockey, 212 anonymous edits

Act_of_Parliament *Source*: http://en.wikipedia.org/w/index.php?title=Act_of_Parliament *Contributors*: Abou Ben Adhem, Acather96, Alex756, Alinor, Alistair1978, Alphaboi867, Altermike, Amlder20, Andrew Gray, Andrew Gwilliam, Andy Marchbanks, Angela, Angusmclellan, Apau98, Arctic.gnome, ArielGold, Astrotrain, Aximrules, Bidgee, Bodnotbod, Bonás, Boyswish, Breadandcheese, Bryan Derksen, Bulwersator, Cahk, CanadianLinuxUser, Capecodeph, Chrism, Chuunen Baka, Cutler, Cybercobra, D.M. from Ukraine, Dan Allen, David Newton, Ddye, Deano wig, Douglas the Comeback Kid, Eddpayne, Elano, Epsilon60198, Espoo, Evercat, Ewanduffy, Filippowiki, Francis Davey, G2bambino, GSlicer, Gabbe, Galoubet, George Burgess, Glane23, Ground Zero, Hairy Dude, Henrygb, Ignasv, InverseHypercube, Jabencarsey, JackLumber, JackofOz, James500, Jdforrester, JeremyR, Jncraton, JonathanFreed, Jprg1966, KJS77, Kaal, Keilana, Kurando, Leandrod, Ling.Nut, Linkoman, Linmhall, Liyang, Lockesdonkey, Lord Emsworth, Lyndafis, Mac, Mais oui!, Marnanel, MartinHarper, Materialscientist, Mauls, Maximus Rex, Miesianiacal, Mindmatrix, Minna Sora no Shita, Mintguy, Mnmazur, Montrealais, Morwen, Mr Gronk, Naddy, Nazi 2007, Nightkey, Ninetyone, NorthernThunder, NoychoH, Obey, Obli, Orcano, Owain, Petrb, Philip Stevens, Phương Huy, Pmyteh, PoliSciMaster, PullUpYourSocks, Rborek, Reaper Eternal, Renata, RetiredUser2, Reuvenk, Riana, Ricardo monteiro, Richard75, Road Wizard, Roadrunner, Rossami, Ryan, SD6-Agent, SGBailey, Saccerzd, Sfan00 IMG, Sionnach1, Sjorford, Smalljim, Smurfandbuffalo, Smyth, Splash, StanZegel, THEN WHO WAS PHONE?, Tabletop, TaerkastUA, TimBentley, Timeshift9, TreasuryTag, TreveX, Tzartzam, Vardion, WTM, Wafulz, Wasbeer, Wik, Wilsonjtd, Wjmcba, Wmahan, Zymurgy, 151 anonymous edits

Burial_Laws_Amendment_Act_1880 *Source*: http://en.wikipedia.org/w/index.php?title=Burial_Laws_Amendment_Act_1880 *Contributors*: Dthomsen8, James500, Tim!, Yutsi

Image Sources, Licenses and Contributors

File:Parliament at night.JPG *Source*: http://en.wikipedia.org/w/index.php?title=File:Parliament_at_night.JPG *License*: unknown *Contributors*: Riaz Shah

File:Palace of Westminster, London - Feb 2007.jpg *Source*: http://en.wikipedia.org/w/index.php?title=File:Palace_of_Westminster,_London_-_Feb_2007.jpg *License*: unknown *Contributors*: User:Diliff

File:Stormont Parliamentary Building 01.JPG *Source*: http://en.wikipedia.org/w/index.php?title=File:Stormont_Parliamentary_Building_01.JPG *License*: unknown *Contributors*: Ardfern, Cnyborg, Savh, Wknight94, 2 anonymous edits

File:Parliament portcullis.png *Source*: http://en.wikipedia.org/w/index.php?title=File:Parliament_portcullis.png *License*: unknown *Contributors*: Barryob, Calmer Waters, Cloudbound, Gaimhreadhan, Nat, Nehrams2020, Seth Whales

File:House of Commons.jpg *Source*: http://en.wikipedia.org/w/index.php?title=File:House_of_Commons.jpg *License*: unknown *Contributors*: UK Parliament

File:Australian House of Representatives - Parliament of Australia.jpg *Source*: http://en.wikipedia.org/w/index.php?title=File:Australian_House_of_Representatives_-_Parliament_of_Australia.jpg *License*: unknown *Contributors*: User:JJ Harrison

File:Unibicameral Map.svg *Source*: http://en.wikipedia.org/w/index.php?title=File:Unibicameral_Map.svg *License*: unknown *Contributors*: User:SkyBon

File:Scottish Parliament, Main Debating Chamber - geograph.org.uk - 1650829.jpg *Source*: http://en.wikipedia.org/w/index.php?title=File:Scottish_Parliament,_Main_Debating_Chamber_-_geograph.org.uk_-_1650829.jpg *License*: unknown *Contributors*: Man vyi, Nobelium, Rock drum

File:Reykjavik althing.jpg *Source*: http://en.wikipedia.org/w/index.php?title=File:Reykjavik_althing.jpg *License*: unknown *Contributors*: User:Wars

File:20070124 sejm sala plenarna.jpg *Source*: http://en.wikipedia.org/w/index.php?title=File:20070124_sejm_sala_plenarna.jpg *License*: unknown *Contributors*: VaGla, Yarl, 2 anonymous edits

File:Daoiz o Velarde.jpg *Source*: http://en.wikipedia.org/w/index.php?title=File:Daoiz_o_Velarde.jpg *License*: unknown *Contributors*: Epaminondas Pantulis

File:houses.of.parliament.overall.arp.jpg *Source*: http://en.wikipedia.org/w/index.php?title=File:Houses.of.parliament.overall.arp.jpg *License*: unknown *Contributors*: Arpingstone, Bhoeble, Common Good, Mtaylor848, Nichtbesserwisser, Tacsipacsi, 1 anonymous edits

File:Parliament-Ottawa.jpg *Source*: http://en.wikipedia.org/w/index.php?title=File:Parliament-Ottawa.jpg *License*: unknown *Contributors*: User:Arctic.gnome

File:Reichstag mit Wiese2.jpg *Source*: http://en.wikipedia.org/w/index.php?title=File:Reichstag_mit_Wiese2.jpg *License*: unknown *Contributors*: -jha-, BLueFiSH.as, Beek100, CGN2010, MB-one, Warburg

File:Palazzo Montecitorio Rom 2009.jpg *Source*: http://en.wikipedia.org/w/index.php?title=File:Palazzo_Montecitorio_Rom_2009.jpg *License*: unknown *Contributors*: User:Manfred Heyde

File:House of Parlament, Budapest, Hungary.JPG *Source*: http://en.wikipedia.org/w/index.php?title=File:House_of_Parlament,_Budapest,_Hungary.JPG *License*: unknown *Contributors*: SveMir (Svetlana i Mirko)

File:Austrian Parliament Building by night.jpg *Source*: http://en.wikipedia.org/w/index.php?title=File:Austrian_Parliament_Building_by_night.jpg *License*: unknown *Contributors*: User:MRB

File:Jatiyo Sangshad Bhaban (Roehl).jpg *Source*: http://en.wikipedia.org/w/index.php?title=File:Jatiyo_Sangshad_Bhaban_(Roehl).jpg *License*: unknown *Contributors*: Karl Ernst Roehl (ke.roehl AT web.de)

File:Portuguese Parliament building front fachade.jpg *Source*: http://en.wikipedia.org/w/index.php?title=File:Portuguese_Parliament_building_front_fachade.jpg *License*: unknown *Contributors*: Andrés Monroy-Hernández from Cambridge, USA

File:Diet of Japan Kokkai 2009.jpg *Source*: http://en.wikipedia.org/w/index.php?title=File:Diet_of_Japan_Kokkai_2009.jpg *License*: unknown *Contributors*: User:Wiiii

File:SansadBhavan.jpg *Source*: http://en.wikipedia.org/w/index.php?title=File:SansadBhavan.jpg *License*: unknown *Contributors*: Bill Strong from Melbourne, Australia

Image:Pakistani parliament house.jpg *Source*: http://en.wikipedia.org/w/index.php?title=File:Pakistani_parliament_house.jpg *License*: unknown *Contributors*: User Waqas.usman on en.wikipedia

File:Verkhovna Rada Ukrainy.jpg *Source*: http://en.wikipedia.org/w/index.php?title=File:Verkhovna_Rada_Ukrainy.jpg *License*: unknown *Contributors*: Jurij Skoblenko aka Olduser

File:BeirutParliament.jpg *Source*: http://en.wikipedia.org/w/index.php?title=File:BeirutParliament.jpg *License*: unknown *Contributors*: Chesdovi, Heretiq, Kilom691, Qasamaan

File:2005-04-27 Koweït 003.jpg *Source*: http://en.wikipedia.org/w/index.php?title=File:2005-04-27_Koweït_003.jpg *License*: unknown *Contributors*: User:Leshonai

File:Book of common prayer 1549.jpg *Source*: http://en.wikipedia.org/w/index.php?title=File:Book_of_common_prayer_1549.jpg *License*: unknown *Contributors*: Original uploader was Ptolemy Caesarion at en.wikipedia

File:Book of common prayer 1552.jpg *Source*: http://en.wikipedia.org/w/index.php?title=File:Book_of_common_prayer_1552.jpg *License*: unknown *Contributors*: Ptolemy Caesarion, Stefan2

File:Book of common prayer 1559.jpg *Source*: http://en.wikipedia.org/w/index.php?title=File:Book_of_common_prayer_1559.jpg *License*: unknown *Contributors*: Ptolemy Caesarion, Stefan2

File:Book of common prayer Scotland 1637.jpg *Source*: http://en.wikipedia.org/w/index.php?title=File:Book_of_common_prayer_Scotland_1637.jpg *License*: unknown *Contributors*: Calliopejen1, Dave souza, Ptolemy Caesarion, Stefan2

File:Book of common prayer 1662.jpg *Source*: http://en.wikipedia.org/w/index.php?title=File:Book_of_common_prayer_1662.jpg *License*: unknown *Contributors*: Ptolemy Caesarion, Stefan2

File:1689 Prayerbook Collect for 5 November.jpg *Source*: http://en.wikipedia.org/w/index.php?title=File:1689_Prayerbook_Collect_for_5_November.jpg *License*: unknown *Contributors*: Unknown: Scan by Steven J Plunkett, 2008

File:Edward Bouverie Pusey.jpg *Source*: http://en.wikipedia.org/w/index.php?title=File:Edward_Bouverie_Pusey.jpg *License*: unknown *Contributors*: -

File:Book of Common Prayers in a Church in Sagda.jpg *Source*: http://en.wikipedia.org/w/index.php?title=File:Book_of_Common_Prayers_in_a_Church_in_Sagda.jpg *License*: unknown *Contributors*: Jayzl Nebre-Villafania

File:Book of Common Prayer Chinese-English Diglot.jpg *Source*: http://en.wikipedia.org/w/index.php?title=File:Book_of_Common_Prayer_Chinese-English_Diglot.jpg *License*: unknown *Contributors*: User:Nasugbu batangas

File:Legislative procedure uk.svg *Source*: http://en.wikipedia.org/w/index.php?title=File:Legislative_procedure_uk.svg *License*: unknown *Contributors*: ╟─TreasuryTag►hemicycle─╢. Original uploader was TreasuryTag at en.wikipedia

MIX
Papier aus verantwortungsvollen Quellen
Paper from responsible sources
FSC® C105338

Printed by Books on Demand GmbH, Norderstedt / Germany